Babylon

A Captivating Guide to the Kingdom in Ancient Mesopotamia, Starting from the Akkadian Empire to the Battle of Opis Against Persia, Including Babylonian Mythology and the Legacy of Babylonia

Free Bonus from Captivating History
(Available for a Limited time)

Hi History Lovers!

Now you have a chance to join our exclusive history list so you can get your first history ebook for free as well as discounts and a potential to get more history books for free! Simply visit the link below to join.

Captivatinghistory.com/ebook

Also, make sure to follow us on Facebook, Twitter and Youtube by searching for Captivating History.

Contents

Introduction

When someone hears the word "Babylon," what do they imagine? If the individual is a fan of language, they might envision a paradise filled with luxury and the finest delights. If they enjoy science fiction, they could conjure up numerous movies and TV shows which play upon the word and build upon its cultural connotations to convey a complex picture like the ill-fated *Babylon 5*. Still, someone raised in the Abrahamic religions—Judaism, Christianity, or Islam—might envision a city of depravity which served as a lesson to the faithful to avoid the temptations of the physical world. After all, the Whore of Babylon continues to be an omnipresent figure in popular culture and theological and spiritual discourse.

But what was Babylon?

The short answer: Even in history, it depends on the context. The long answer is more complicated. When someone says Babylon, they could be referring to either a major city, an empire, or an entire group of people which characterized the wider region of Mesopotamia and thousands of years of human history and development. For the purposes of this book, the third definition is used.

The Babylonians were never one static people with a single background but instead developed their civilization over the centuries by incorporating more and more peoples into one great culture. The savvy reader will notice that their history is complex and highly detailed. By the end of this book, readers will be sick of seeing the words "Babylon," "Babylonia," "Babylonian," and "civilization," but they will come away with a greater understanding of just why this culture is considered one of the most significant and influential of all time.

The Babylonian influence upon its successors and even modern society knows no bounds. One of the leading civilizations of Mesopotamia, the Babylonians provided the fundamentals of mathematics, agriculture, architecture, metallurgy, and other influential and necessary fields required to develop other great civilizations such as the Greeks, Romans, and even contemporary nations like China and the United States. Without them, no neoteric world could exist.

Keeping all of this in mind, it's important to place the Babylonians within the proper context, and that means a brief overview about what Mesopotamia was and why so many civilizations get associated or categorized as Babylonian. Since they existed so long ago, the dates referenced will end with BCE, which stands for Before Common Era, or the start of the contemporary Gregorian calendar. So, when a date like 1850 BCE appears, you want to add the current year plus the number 1850 to find how long ago something occurred. For example: 2018 plus 1850 means the event happened 3,868 years in the past. The story of Babylonia begins in what modern scholars define as Mesopotamia, the landmass in between the Euphrates and Tigris Rivers in the Near East.

Chapter 1 – The Land of the Babylonians

The land around the Euphrates River, such as the regions outside of Mesopotamia itself, and in the original Mesopotamia shaped the development of the Babylonian civilization. Ancient Babylonia rested in southern Mesopotamia in the Ancient Near East. For a contemporary audience, this would be roughly the location of modern nations such as Iraq, Iran, Israel, Jordan, Turkey, Syria, Egypt, Palestine, and Saudi Arabia. Although the city of Babylon itself would remain around for centuries, the actual civilization and kingdom of the Babylonians would undergo many name changes as different cultures entered the region and merged with existing ones. For example, in the third millennia BCE, central Mesopotamia was known as Akkad while the southern region was Sumer.

Mesopotamia was the origin of human civilization as contemporary peoples know it. Together with Egypt, to which it was connected by the massive Tigris and Euphrates Rivers, Mesopotamia formed the basis of civilization through the advent of agriculture, writing, mathematics, architecture, and the other building blocks of culture and society. One of the major reasons for the region's success was the presence of diverse peoples and fertile farmland which provided enough sustenance for individuals to focus on other matters besides finding food. Mesopotamia encompasses the geographical region between the Tigris and Euphrates, which received the moisture it needed from the waters of the rivers and provided fertile farmland.

The Tigris River

Akkad or Upper and Central Mesopotamia

This section of Mesopotamia was a vast flatland measuring roughly 250 miles in length. The soil would have been reasonably fertile, but not lush. The flatland only experiences one major disruption, which is a range of limestone that branches off of the nearby Zagros mountain range. Numerous settlements existed in this area during the time of the Babylonians, including major cities and large swathes of farmland used to produce agricultural staples like barley. Archaeologists still find many ruins and remnants of old towns and houses in the area.

To the north of the flatland and past the limestone feature is another section of well-watered country with more limestone hills. More farmland existed in this area, and quarries dotted the region to dig out and carve up the limestone for use in construction. At the very tip of this region was the end of the extent of the Babylonian territory. Here, the Tigris and Euphrates Rivers rose up into the ridges of the Zagros mountain range, which separated the Babylonians and their predecessors from their neighbors. In this area would have been the major city of Asur or Assur, as well as the future capital of Nineveh even farther north.

Sumer or Lower Mesopotamia

The lower segment of Mesopotamia contained alluvial plains designed for rich agriculture. This area was called Chaldea and was fertilized by the rich deposits left by the Tigris and Euphrates. Several sections of this book will reference the Chaldeans, who are frequently considered to be part of the Babylonian Empire—they were just one of many smaller ethnic groups which formed broader Mesopotamia and the empire itself. To the east is the mountain range of Elam while the west holds the banks of the Euphrates, which separated Mesopotamia from a group of nomadic peoples called the Suti. These Suti did not come from the same general background as the Chaldeans (who were Babylonians) and were one of many Semitic language speaking peoples that dotted the area. Along the south of the Mesopotamian territory were sea marshes where many of the Chaldeans lived alongside other ethnic groups like the Arameans and Kaldy.[1]

Various cities dotted the landscape. To the west of the territory was the famous Ur, the first capital of Mesopotamia and perhaps the oldest known city in existence. It's from this city that the phrase "Ur example" originates, which means the first incidence of something. Babylon rested to the west and possessed numerous suburbs on both sides of the Euphrates. Also in this area were considerable red sandstone deposits and cliffs from which the Babylonians took stone, as well as a freshwater sea called Najaf.

---

[1] Bill T. Arnold, *Who Were the Babylonians?*, (Atlanta: The Society of Biblical Literature, 2004).

5

The Ruins of Babylon – 1932 Photograph

On the east bank of the Euphrates and to the south of Babylon were the significant cities of Kish and Nippur, which would play an important role in the development of a cohesive civilization. To the east was the Lagash channel that allowed access across the Tigris River. This channel would set the stage for Babylonian conquest and expansion at its neighbors' expense.

It was in this same area that the Sumerians and Akkadians, the Babylonians' ancestors, also developed. When examining the Babylonians, it's impossible not to look at the other two. This is because they were other cultures and ethnic groups which would contribute significantly to the Babylonians' science, religion, and societal structure. When the Babylonian Empire formed, the Sumerians and Akkadians didn't disappear so much as become absorbed into the new civilization and became members of the encompassing term "Babylonian." The same would happen to the Chaldeans and other smaller groups. The absorption or assimilation occurred when the Babylonian ancestors, the Amorites, arrived in the region and started to practice intermarriage and assimilation of their own.

When Did the Babylonians Live?

The Babylonians are one of the oldest known organized civilizations, dating back to the 19th century BCE.[2] The civilization would last until the Islamic conquests in the 700s CE, meaning some form of the Babylonians was in existence for a continuous 2,500 years. The Babylonians would have started during the end of the Mesopotamian Bronze Age (3500 BCE – 1500 BCE). This meant that the Babylonians possessed the technology required to craft weapons and tools from bronze, a soft metal that was stronger than original models made of stone. They then transitioned to the Iron Age, where bronze was replaced by the even tougher iron.

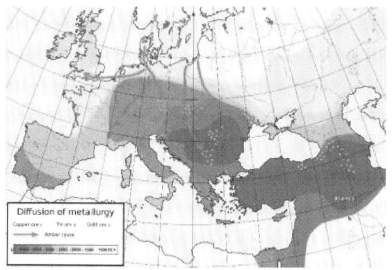

The Diffusion of Metallurgy

The picture above shows how the region in which the Babylonians lived was one of the first areas to develop metallurgy and bronze weaponry. For this reason, Mesopotamia is frequently called the "cradle of civilization." Access to and knowledge of bronze metallurgy meant the Babylonians were capable of dominating other areas that had not yet acquired such technology. In essence, it gave

[2] Paul Kriwaczek, *Babylon: Mesopotamia and the Birth of Civilization*, (New York: St. Martin's Press, 2012).

them an advantage that allowed the civilization to thrive. It was in this environment that the Babylonians started their journey that would go down in the annals of history.

Chapter 2 – Life, Culture, and Gender Roles Throughout the Years

Considering the Babylonians developed over two and a half millennia, their culture varied greatly. However, ancient civilizations also didn't experience changes as quickly as many modern societies, and historians and archaeologists are unable to track more minute developments such as favorite foods or outfits in each century. On a large level, historians do know that Babylonia was characterized by the same militaristic monarchy of other civilizations, meaning there was usually a warrior king supported by some wealthy nobles who took positions as generals, priests, and administrators. The economy was driven mainly through trade, but the majority of individuals would have worked as farmers trying to grow enough food for themselves and their families. This chapter provides a broad overview of what the average Babylonian, those farmers and sometimes traders, would consider daily life, including gender roles, potential jobs, and the kind of food that could have been eaten.

The Role of Men and Women

Men dominated the public sphere of the Babylonian world. They were the primary holders of property, the heads of households and families, and were all expected to work outside of the home. They could be free men who worked in the military or government, and they formed the majority of the labor force. Some sample work a typical man might do could be planting and harvesting crops, constructing buildings and bridges, recording administrative records, fighting as a soldier, or brewing beer. Because they controlled the public sphere, men were seen as the "standard" citizens. Their opinions mattered more than those of women and children, and they held the ultimate control over their wives and children. Although women could be influential, the Babylonian world was dominated by men.

Almost everything to do within the home was considered women's work, as well as the gathering and refining of materials. Some scholars summarize the separation of the genders best by describing the role of the man as the provider of raw materials like grain and wool, while the role of the woman was to take these goods and create a finished product like bread or fabric for clothing. Since women maintained the home, they also needed to go out every day and draw water from a nearby river, canal, or stream. One of their main tasks was the gathering of firewood as well, which could be obtained by picking up dropped sticks or chopping branches from nearby trees.

Sumerian and Babylonian texts from the third and second millennia BCE indicate that women did work outside of the home, usually as domestic servants and laborers for merchants and wealthier families. The Babylonians appeared to pay laborers with either silver or barley, which was administered based on a person's age and gender. For example, a man who worked for a month could receive 190 cups of barley, while a woman would receive 139.[3] Although there was definitely a fair amount of misogyny involved since women were not as valued as men; the chief reason the Babylonians paid men more was because they required more food. Even though women also performed backbreaking labor, they were able to get by with less nutrition and food consumed than a man of equivalent size.

Interestingly, if there were severe agricultural issues, such as poor harvests, employers would pay laborers with less barley but would make up the difference with dates. For example, a woman might receive only 84.5 cups of barley but would then be given 13 dates as well. Still, even when employers paid in silver, women received only

---

[3] Marten Stol, *Women in the Ancient Near East,* (Boston: De Gruyter, 2016), pg. 342.

one-third of the wages of men and sometimes even only one-fourth. Some historians speculate that part of the difference occurred because men, being naturally stronger, could do harder labor, but all agree that the low Babylonian opinion of women played a significant role.

So, what was the kind of work men and women did? Men could develop specialized skills to become merchants and craftsmen, but the majority were poor farmers who spent their days toiling in the fields, digging furrows, planting crops, and then harvesting them at the end of the season. Some wealthier individuals could become rudimentary blacksmiths who made tools and weapons while others bought and sold goods. Many men dedicated their lives to the military and became soldiers, though poorer individuals were not well-equipped and would often die in battle. If a man could become educated, he might become an administrator that kept records and worked with the king and nobility, but he would have to be noble himself. Finally, many men worked as poor day laborers and construction workers who were employed by the month.

As for the women, many of their duties involved taking materials and turning them into something useful. Besides weaving, grinding wheat, and baking, women also dug trenches for canals, laid building foundations, built sluices, made the furrows in fields for crops, gathered harvests, pressed oil, and carried materials like bricks to construction sites. Records indicate that a free woman could be obliged to become a slave worker for a period of time for which her husband would be paid with a small plot of land. The wife did not have a say in her employment. In addition, women held primary responsibilities when it came to raising and educating children. It was common for a mother to labor during the day and bring her children with her, where they would then become child workers who earned meager wages.

Marriage, Sexuality, Family, and Divorce

For the majority of Babylonians, marriage was the most important event in an individual's life. Many rituals, laws, and cultural practices surrounded the engagement, wedding, and then following covenant of marriage between a man and woman. For men, the average age of marriage would be between 18 and 20. For women, a young girl could expect to be married shortly after she got her first period, usually between 13 and 14. This age of marriage for women did create some problems since maternal mortality rates during and after childbirth were extremely high. Although the girls had gotten their periods, their bodies were frequently not fully developed, and they therefore suffered greatly when trying to have children.

Marriage was one of the most essential institutions for the Babylonians, and numerous ancient texts praise marriage going back over a period of 3,000 years. Religious texts decreed that it was the ultimate destiny of men and women to form happy pairs that produced healthy children. A satisfying sex life was seen as central to this institution, and religious and cultural sources encouraged husbands and wives to find joy in one another's arms. Early Babylonian (officially Sumerian) proverbs explained these ideas, as did the depiction of female demons who were unable to experience the pleasure of marriage and children. One proverb went thusly:

May Inanna let a wife with hot hips lie down with you. May she present you with sons with broad arms. May she search out a place of happiness for you.[4]

A "wife with hot hips" refers to a woman who is sexually aroused. The Babylonians believed an aroused woman who orgasmed was more fertile and thus more likely to have healthy children, especially sons. Something that might come as a surprise to a modern audience was how candid the Babylonians were about sexuality. Women were expected to be virgins upon marriage and men were not, but both married individuals were expected to enjoy one another and have sex frequently. Indeed, it was seen as the most common activity of a happy, healthy living individual, which is why the demons of the Babylonian religion were so evil—they never got to experience life as an accomplished woman. Their description was as follows, and shows just how important marriage and sex was seen for the average woman:

The maiden is like a woman who never had intercourse.

The maiden is like a woman who was never deflowered.

The maiden never experienced sex in her husband's life.

The maiden never peeled off her clothes on her husband's lap.

---

[4] Sumerian Proverbs 1.147.

The maiden's clasp no nice-looking lad ever loosened.

The maiden had no milk in her breasts; only bitter liquid exudes.

The maiden never climaxed sexually, nor satisfied her desires in a man's lap.[5]

Likewise, a man's life without marriage was seen as empty and barren. However, this doesn't mean that romantic love was encouraged. Marriage for the Babylonians, as with many ancient civilizations, was transactional. For an engagement to take place, a man had to come to an agreement with his future father-in-law about a marriage price. He would bestow gifts upon his intended betrothed and paid a set amount to her father before the marriage could take place.

If the future husband and wife were both free individuals and not slaves, then the wedding consisted of the woman being delivered to her future husband's house. He would place a veil upon her head and cover her face, declaring that she was his wife. After this, he would pour perfume over her head and then present her with gifts. Once married, the couple needed to decide future living arrangements. Sometimes the new wife would return to live with her father. If this were the case, the husband would give her a payment known as a *dumaki*, which went toward the maintenance of the house. If the couple chose to live together, the wife would bring a *sherigtu* with her, or the equivalent of a dowry.

This *sherigtu* was entirely the wife's property and could not be claimed by her husband's brothers if the husband died. Likewise, she got to keep any marriage presents given to her by her husband, such as jewelry. However, if the wife died without having any children, then the price her husband paid for her needed to be returned to him. If the husband chose to divorce his wife, then he owed the former father-in-law satisfaction, usually some amount of money.

Babylonian men typically only took one wife if she lived and produced children, especially male heirs. However, it was perfectly legal for men to enter more than one marriage or engage in relations with a concubine to try to have more children. Although it was allowed, it culturally wasn't accepted if the husband was not noble

---

[5] Stol, *Women in the Ancient Near East,* pg. 61.

or had a wife who did produce children and survived. If a man did take a concubine, she was incorporated into the household but could only wear a veil, the symbol of a married woman, outside when walking with the wife. Her position in the household would always be inferior to the legal wife, and the concubine was usually chosen from the slaves.

Once children were born to a married couple, the husband then became a father and the head of the household. He retained the power of life and death over his wife and offspring. Some of his powers included leaving children with creditors as security for the repayment of a debt, sending them to work, and choosing whom to leave money and property too—although the eldest son also retained some rights. If the man died, his sons could claim his property and kick their mother out of the home, but they might need to fight their uncles.

Finally, there was the possibility of divorce. Surprisingly, the Babylonian law codes did eventually allow for women to initiate a divorce. In particular, laws appeared in codes dictated by the famous Hammurabi. If a woman could provide evidence of severe abuse or neglect on the part of her husband, then she was free to leave his home and return to that of her parents. Meanwhile, a man could initiate a divorce for two main reasons: his wife proved to be infertile or was accused of adultery. No one suspected that a man could be infertile.

However, divorce was heavily stigmatized, and the husband would always have to return the dowry he received from the marriage. To avoid social ostracizing, most unhappy couples remained together. Husbands usually added a concubine to the family or started affairs, and women would carry out their own illicit activities in secret.

Adultery was a punishable offense for women and their lovers. Babylonian law dictated that a cuckolded husband could have his unfaithful wife and her lover or lovers thrown in the river to drown. If he wished to spare his wife, then he also had to let her lover go. Punishment for adultery was all or nothing. Married men were not punished for carrying out affairs unless they were caught with a married woman who was not his wife.[6]

---

[6] Ibid.

Now, this is an overview of the general structure of Babylonian marriage and divorce throughout three millennia. Naturally, Sumerian, Akkadian, and then official Babylonian men and women would have different levels of power and slightly changed social norms depending on which culture held the most influence and power at a given time. The most major change that can be seen over the millennia was the diminishing role of women. While the Sumerians gave women unprecedented power in the ancient world to leave an unhappy marriage and home, and even depicted women as having incredible power over their husbands, this rapidly changed under the Akkadians and the Babylonians.

Food

Modern historians and archaeologists know a great deal about Babylonian cuisine because chefs preserved their recipes on clay tablets which were then discovered many millennia later. From these tablets, it can be discerned that one of the most common foods eaten by the Babylonians was stew. A stew could be made from all of the leftovers and bits found by wives and slaves in their households and then preserved for days by being left in the heat. Some common ingredients for stew included meat, hardy vegetables, and locally found herbs.

The meats could be from any of the common animals shepherded by locals. These included mutton (sheep meat), pork, poultry, fish, and some beef. However, most people did not eat meat often since it was difficult and costly to raise an animal to only slaughter it for meat. A commoner would be lucky to have some form of meat once a week. Onions were the most common vegetable, and garlic could be used as seasoning.[7]

Bread made from barley was the primary staple of the Babylonian diet. Barley could be grown in a variety of environments found throughout the Babylonian territory and provided efficient nutrition. Men would frequently be the harvesters of barley and would bring the grain to women, who would spend hours grinding it down with a mortar and pestle. Afterward, they would take the flour to make dough that could be cooked into flat loaves eaten for dinner.

---

[7] "Publications," Yale University Babylonian Collection, Yale University, last modified 2018, https://babylonian-collection.yale.edu/publications.

Accompanying the barley bread was often locally grown fruits such as figs, plums, melons, and dates.

The drink of choice was beer made from excess barley rather than wine. This beer would not be the same as modern beer. Instead, it had a lower alcohol content to make it more palatable and drinkable throughout the day. The primary reason the Babylonians drank beer was to avoid becoming sick from drinking river water, especially since the river was used for bathing, washing clothes, and often using the bathroom. Both men and women were involved in the manufacture of barley beer.

In 2018, a collaborative team from Yale University and Harvard University gathered information from existing cuneiform clay tablets and attempted to reconstruct and make several ancient Babylonian recipes. Two prominent scholars helped head the team, Agnete Lassen and Chelsea Alene Graham. Lassen was the associate curator of the Yale Babylonian Collection while Graham was the digital imaging specialist for the Institute of the Preservation of Cultural Heritage.[8] Their goal was to develop three separate stews. Recreating the meals was difficult as the tablets were poorly preserved, some ingredients were not available, and there were no measurements. The results, however, were delicious.

Language

The Babylonians used a language known as Akkadian, which they took from their predecessors the Akkadians. No one speaks this language any longer as it was an ancient Semitic tongue written in a cuneiform script. Cuneiform was an early system of writing developed by Sumerians. It featured many wedge-shaped symbols which represented different spoken syllables. The symbols were made by pressing a reed into wet clay, which could then be erased. Sometimes, scribes baked the tablets to preserve the writing. The heat from the ovens would harden the clay, forming hard slabs that could then be passed to other scholars or educated members of society—usually the nobility or wealthy merchants.

---

[8] Bess Connolly Martell, "What Did Ancient Babylonians Eat? A Yale-Harvard Team Tested Their Recipes," YaleNews, last modified 2018, https://news.yale.edu/2018/06/14/what-did-ancient-babylonians-eat-yale-harvard-team-tested-their-recipes.

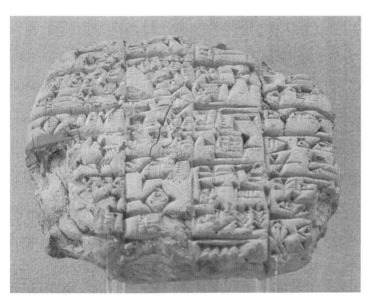

A Cuneiform Letter, c. 2400 BCE

Buildings and Architecture

Despite the civilization's age, the Babylonians are known for their art and general creativity when it comes to building and architecture. For instance, instead of the traditional square or rectangular bricks, the Babylonians made bricks with rounded edges. These bricks weren't the most stable but were aesthetically pleasing and contributed to the unique look of structures like the ziggurat, a type of temple.

According to one older historian by the name of Archibald Sayce, the most common building materials for homes and temples were still stone and brick. In one of his monographs, he describes Babylonian architecture as follows:

Stone was scarce, but was already cut into blocks and seals. Brick was the ordinary building material, and with it cities, forts, temples and houses were constructed. The city was provided with towers and stood on an artificial platform; the house also had a tower-like appearance. It was provided with a door which turned on a hinge, and could be opened with a sort of key; the city gate was on a larger scale, and seems to have been double. ... Demons were feared who had wings like a bird, and the foundation stones – or rather bricks – of a house were consecrated by certain objects that were deposited under them.[9]

His descriptions match modern interpretations. Most Babylonian buildings were built on slightly raised platforms to keep dust and dirt out of the house and prevent flooding during the rainy season. Mud bricks were the most common building material because they were simple, cheap, and plentiful. Stone was reserved for the wealthy or for influential edifices such as the central temples of the cities, including the famous ziggurats. Most buildings did not use mortar, the material that keeps bricks together. Instead, the Babylonians relied on the weight of the bricks and the skill of their architecture to keep structures standing. In the cases of temples and palaces, large buttresses were used.

Other notable architectural features were drains used to keep water and runoff away from the bases of buildings. These drains could be as simple as dirt ditches or as elaborate as large half-pipes made of lead. Many bricks could be plated as time went on, with etchings or thin layers of gold for decoration. Frescoes and wall decorations additionally appeared as art developed. Walls were almost never plain and were frequently painted in bright, vibrant colors through the use of plant dyes. Some common colors appear to be the basic yellow and blue that could be made from wildflowers and berries.

The Babylonians were also one of the first Mesopotamian civilizations to step away from the traditional bas-relief. A bas-relief was a sculpture carved into a massive section of stone. It wasn't an engraving, but rather an elaborate image that was given some three-dimensional shape and development by cutting around the desired image. Instead of these bas-reliefs, the Babylonians started to create fully three-dimensional statues that stood alone. This was because stone was considered a precious and finite resource, and it was important not to waste material by only cutting out part of an image and leaving so much stone behind to form a backdrop.

---

[9] Rev. A.H. Sayce, Professor of Assyriology, Oxford, "The Archaeology of the Cuneiform Inscriptions", *Society for Promoting Christian Knowledge*, 1908, pgs. 98–100

An Assyrian Bas-Relief from 716-713 BCE

Clothing

It's difficult to tell what the Babylonians personally wore since not many depictions survived the sands of time. Archaeologists and historians can tell that most of the Babylonian wardrobe seemed borrowed wholesale from the Sumerians. This meant that both men and women typically wore outfits made from sewn fabric that formed medium to long skirts and shawls. These skirts typically went to a man's knees or a woman's ankles and had some form of fringe around the hem that was plain or elaborate depending on a person's wealth or status. The skirt was held in place by a thick woven belt that was tied in the back to keep the front lines of the garment neat and clean. Since the majority of individuals were poor laborers, clothing was typically the dirty white or brown of undyed wool.[10]

The shawls were long pieces of fabric that could be wrapped around

---

[10] Mary G. Houston, *Ancient Egyptian, Mesopotamian & Persian Costume,* (London: A. & C. Black, 1954).

a person's shoulders to cover the breasts and parts of the shoulders. Women, although modest, did appear to be allowed to show the area around the collarbone in a manner similar to contemporary V-neck tops. As time went on, women started to replace the more traditional skirt and shawl combo with long woolen dresses that went to their feet and could be cinched around the waist with belts. Many continued to wear shawls on top for modesty and added decoration.

Almost all women were required by custom to cover their heads with a veil for modesty. The only ones who did not were slaves who were not seen as deserving the status implied by the presence of a veil. Men did not have the same obligation, but frequently wore some form of covering as protection from the sun while out farming or trading. Their most distinctive feature was the presence of long, carefully curled beards that indicated a man was an adult. Most individuals wore a form of sandal as protection from the ground, while soldiers and the nobility could afford high-quality leather boots.

Both genders wore jewelry, which was highly prized. The king typically wore an elaborate hairnet woven from gold strands, while wealthier nobles could afford to use golden ribbons in their hair. The most prized pieces were gold earrings, which could be shaped like crosses, walnuts, or simple rings. People also wore bracelets, necklaces, and bands that featured woven religious symbols, flowers, and even animals like birds. Not everyone could afford jewelry, but even commoners used simple woven pieces as decorations and status symbols.

Chapter 3 – Where Superstition Met Science

Numerous members of a modern audience frequently scoff at the idea of ancient civilizations being technologically advanced, but such individuals often forget that every human must build from the ground up. Simply speaking, someone can't go to college without first having attended kindergarten. This analogy is by no means meant to cheapen the advancements of the Babylonians. It takes a keen mind to be able to chart the heavens and determine how to properly size the area of a geometric shape. Could any of this volume's readers do it if they hadn't been taught the formulas in school?

Out of the various academic fields, the areas where the Babylonians excelled were mathematics and astronomy or astrology, which built off of one another. However, they also failed in some important ones. For example, the Babylonians did not have a good concept of anatomy, physiology, virology, or basic medicine. Instead, many of their methods relied on superstitions to work out a cure, and death was disturbingly common even among individuals who had seen a physician.

Medicine

Babylonian medicine included more superstition than science. Physicians left records of the most common and popular cures on clay tablets, but many of the ingredients involved would have had little to no effect on the diseases or ailments they were supposed to treat. Some could actually make an individual sicker than planned. Anatomy was also not well understood. Although physicians and professionals called diviners would dissect deceased humans and animals to examine their organs, they didn't know what each one did. For example, the liver was considered the most important and the source of the body's blood. Songs even included the liver in place of where a modern audience might use the heart.

A Babylonian physician would devise treatments for a broad range of issues such as respiratory diseases, infections, mental illnesses that caused sadness or hallucinations, poor circulation, trouble conceiving a child, and epilepsy. However, their diagnoses had almost nothing to do with the body. If there was a physical problem with an individual, physicians thought there was a supernatural cause, usually disfavor with a god or the work of evil spirits. With this in mind, physicians frequently created treatments also based in superstition.

One famous example includes the sighting of pigs. If, while on the way to treat a patient, a physician spied a white pig, then the patient would recover. If they spotted a black pig, the patient was doomed. Other colors possessed different meanings as well. The physician might also look at the color of a patient's urine to check for problems. If the urine came out black, then the individual would die—as they would in modern times, usually, so the Babylonians were correct here. Clear urine was usually a sign of recovery, while red or bloody urine meant the illness was severe, but recovery was possible. This sounds like a rudimentary understanding of some common issues related to the bladder and kidneys, which would be prone to infections from poor sanitation and hygiene.

Physicians manufactured their own medicines and also performed surgeries. There was no anesthetic so anyone who needed work done would be in a lot of pain before, during, and after. One potential practice was giving the patient alcohol to keep them numb and distracted. Medicine could be a salve, potion, rubbing oil, a coated wrap, and even enemas. They included a combination of rare and mundane ingredients. Some recipes taken from tablets included:

Heat in premium beer nlnu, mountain plant, hasu, nuhurtu, juniper, kukru, sumlalu, ballukku, cuttings of aromatics, field-clod, plants – filter and cool them, add oil into the mixture – pour it into his anus and he will recover.[11]

This particular cure was for excessive flatulence and bloating. Other medicines could have been for something called sun disease, which was most likely sunburn, and what the Babylonians considered kidney disease. Their kidney disease was characterized by discolored urine and the frequent need to pee, so they were actually quite close to the truth.

The Babylonian system of healthcare was codified and made official during the time of Hammurabi. Laws were made official by being inscribed on the Code of Hammurabi, which was made around 1750 BCE and carved out of an 8 ft. tall piece of black diorite. Some of the laws included:

If the doctor has treated a man for a severe wound with lances of bronze and has caused the man to die, or has opened an abscess of the eye for a man and has caused the loss of the man's eye, one shall cut off his hands.

If a doctor has treated the severe wound of a slave of a poor man with a bronze lances and has caused his death, he shall render slave for slave.

If he has opened his abscess with a bronze lances and has made him lose his eye, he shall pay money, half his price.

If a doctor has cured the shattered limb of a gentleman, or has cured the diseased bowel, the patient shall give five shekels of silver to the doctor.[12]

---

[11] Medical Tablet

[12] Medical Tablet

The Top of the Hammurabi Code

Being a physician was a dangerous profession. If something went wrong—and considering the cures, this would have happened often—then the physician could be mutilated or killed as punishment. There was no such thing as revoking a license.

A sick individual could also contact an exorcist. Since physical complaints were thought to be caused by a supernatural force, it wasn't uncommon for someone to seek out spiritual help. The exorcist's job was to drive away any bad spirits that might be hanging around an individual and causing ailments. This could be done by burning incense or plants, chanting, uttering prayers, or more physical remedies. More often than not, the exorcist would be contacted to deal with a mental health issue, such as hallucinations or chronic anxiety.

Mathematics

The Babylonians understood basic arithmetic and algebra, and even developed tables and tablets designed to provide answers without the user needing to do any complex mathematics. These are similar to the multiplication and division tables given to students in schools around the world today, but these were more sophisticated and capable of solving greater and more finicky equations.

Geometry was also understood. Much of what historians know come from several baked clay tablets which demonstrate some of the mathematical formulas that the Babylonians used for building and measuring the world around them. One of the greatest discoveries was that the Babylonians understood the basic rules necessary to measure the area and volume of multiple shapes. For example, they were able to figure out the circumference of a circle by measuring the diameter and then multiplying by three. They could also figure out the area by squaring the circumference and then dividing by twelve. In essence, these formulas looked like this:

- 3(diameter of the circle) = circumference of the circle

- (Circumference of the circle x circumference of the circle)/12 = area of the circle

Why is this so significant? The Babylonians had figured out the concept of pi or π, and approximated the number by using the easier concept of multiplying by 3. 3 is so close to pi that historians believe its usage was not a coincidence. There is even evidence that the Babylonians were aware that 3 was only an approximation—one Old Babylonian tablet found near Susa actually lists pi as 3.125 instead of 3 but indicates that it's more practical for laborers to simplify the equation for easier calculations. For those unfamiliar with mathematics, 3.125 is only 0.5% lower than the full value of pi. Without pi, numerous facets of architecture would be impossible.

Outside of the circle, the Babylonians also understood how to find the volume of cylinders and similar shapes, and inscribed the correct formulas on their tablets. Surprisingly though, they did not know how to correctly determine the volume of a square pyramid despite building complex structures like the ziggurat.

More impressive was the Babylonian work in the field of astronomy. As mentioned earlier, the civilization featured numerous keen astronomers who kept detailed records of the heavens. Recorded in their tablets was the regular motion of the planets, the directions and angles at which stars rose and set in the sky, when solar and lunar eclipses occurred on the calendar, and how the position of celestial bodies indicated that the world was spherical. The Babylonians even used complex systems like the Fourier analysis to create vast tables of astronomical positions—and the modern Fourier analysis would not be rediscovered until the 1950s.

The Importance of Mathematics

Many understand mathematics to be the building blocks of the world. Without it, humans could not understand how they make their way through physical space, how to calculate distance, how to build solid structures, or how to measure the solids and liquids frequently traded, sold, and consumed throughout time. Or, at least they could not do so accurately.

The Babylonian mathematical discoveries are some of the earliest in existence, predating even the Greeks, whom much of the Western world copied when making "new" scientific discoveries from the medieval period onward. In fact, the Greeks actually wound up copying the work of the Babylonians during the Hellenistic Period, which came over 1,000 years after the Babylonians made their initial discoveries. As far as archaeologists and historians can estimate, Babylonian mathematical knowledge was transferred to Greek civilization following the conquests of Alexander the Great in Mesopotamia and the surrounding region around the 330s BCE.

Alexander the Great, although known for his military triumphs and prowess, additionally emphasized the importance of sharing knowledge and cultural practices. After all, his own soldiers did turn on him after viewing his assimilation into Persian culture as a betrayal to his Macedonian heritage. During his conquest, Alexander ordered Callisthenes of Olynthus, his official chronicler, to compile professionals that would translate the entire body of Babylonian astronomical tables and records.

The Greeks would take these records and make some astonishing discoveries with them that shaped the modern world, including new methods of calculating the calendar and the positions of known planets like Venus and Jupiter. It also facilitated the introduction of complex mathematical concepts further into Hellenistic culture. Some examples of significant mathematical implementations included the Greeks learning to divide a circle into 360 degrees and 60 arc minutes.

Babylonian astrology represents the combination of astronomy with religion. In their worldview, it was as much a science as the calculations indicating where the planets and constellations existed in the sky. The Babylonian, also called Chaldean, astrologers created the foundations of the modern zodiac and heavily influenced their Hellenistic counterparts. Considering how faithfully they mapped the stars and the sheer importance of the deities to everyday life, it should be no surprise to learn that the Babylonians believed the gods would send messages to humans through omens left in the sky.

The Enuma Anu Enlil, Astronomy, and Astrology

The Enuma Anu Enlil is a series of clay tablets written by the Babylonian astrologers in a cuneiform script. It reveals between 6,500 and 7,000 omens that astrologers believed would affect the king or empire in some way or another if they appeared. Some of them were based on real occurrences, but the majority were not. Many translations are currently held in the State Archives of Assyria, which is an intellectual project based in Helsinki, Finland. The entire Enuma Anu Enlil has yet to be translated, and there are numerous gaps in the text from sections where the cuneiform wore thin or disappeared from erosion. Still, it is from here where historians get much of their information about the importance of astrology and divination.

Omens

An omen was a prophetic message which astrologers needed to find and interpret to pass the information along to the priests and king. The Babylonians developed detailed lists of common omens or symbols and their meanings, which were inscribed into traditional clay tablets and then baked for repeated use. An omen could be divided into two parts: the *protasis* and the *apodosis*. Anyone familiar with the craft of writing will recognize these two words, which are based in Greek. The *protasis* was the initial observation and a corresponding hypothesis about the meaning of a symbol. The *apodosis* was the actual outcome of the observed omen. In the tablets, astrologers would keep long lists of seen omens and what happened as a result. In this way, it actually was a form of sophisticated science even if it was built on the wrong assumptions.

Another similarity between Babylonian astrology and science was the presence of theories and hypotheses. The astrologers already exhibited traits of a scientific method of sorts when they tracked an omen and discovered a corresponding event. It was, in its own rudimentary way, simple cause and effect. But the Babylonians went further. Using elements from religious stories, they included in their tablets potential portents or omens and their outcomes. They made hypotheses and theories. However, they had no way to test them, and many of the omens they imagined would have been absolutely impossible considering what humans know now about the laws of nature. But the astrologers still applied fundamental scientific principles to understand the world around them, and this is why Babylonian astrology could be considered a form of science—if not for a modern audience, then for the Babylonians themselves.

To understand omens, one must understand the Babylonian worldview. Although religion is covered in depth later on, it's important to know that the Babylonians existed in a deeply religious society where deities were not static figures. Instead, they were active participants in daily life. The will and favor of the divine resulted in tangible and physical benefits on earth. Even more intriguing was the concept that the earth and the heavens were connected in a sphere. Think of a ball. To the Babylonians, the earth would be the lower half and the sky the upper. All around the edge were connections between the two. Not the atmospheric ones known in contemporary society, but actual physical points of contact. This is because in the Babylonian religion, the goddess Tiamat had been rent in two and used to form the heavens and earth.

With all of this in mind, omens could be considered the gods writing messages on the upper half of the world, and it was therefore the task of humans down below to discern the meaning. Even once this meaning was found, the future was not set. This concept was common among the ancient civilizations of the Near East and northern Africa. Even if the Babylonians found an omen, it did not mean that the event would happen. It was actually a judgment of the gods who, in their wisdom, had seen what could happen and chose to pass the information to the Babylonians. The gods gave, in the words of French historian Jean Bottéro, "a verdict against the interested parties on the basis of the elements in the omen, just as each sentence by a tribunal established the future of the guilty person based upon the dossier submitted to its judgement."[13]

So, once the Babylonian astrologers discovered an omen and interpreted it, they told the results to the king and the priests. It was then the task of these officials to find ways to either prevent or facilitate the outcome. This was done by performing rituals and sacrifices to the relevant deities. To give an example, if the astrologers found a sign indicating that the king was to die soon, he and the high priests would attempt to stop the death from occurring by sacrificing expensive animals like bulls and oxen, anointing the statues of the chief deity as well as the god of the underworld, and performing as many rituals as possible. This could be considered an appeal to the divine high court. Then, the gods would make their judgment. If they were pleased, the king would live. If not, he would die.

The Constellations, Zodiac, and Planets

The Babylonians possessed a complex system for understanding the movements of the planets and the stars. Similar to a modern zodiac, they believed that the positions of certain celestial bodies influenced the world and especially an individual. Depending on the composition of the sky at one's birth, a person would possess different personality traits, characteristics, and fortunes in life.

The Babylonian sky was divided into three main subsections named after the trio of chief deities: Anu, the god of the sky and chief deity; Enlil, the god of weather; and Ea, the god of water. They did not have planets associated with them, but other deities did. The planets were not thought to be the gods, but rather representations or symbols of their power. Planetary positions were associated with specific days, months, and years that were said to be favorable to each deity.[14]

The most important "planets" to the Babylonians were the moon and the sun. For the sun, a special emphasis was placed on its size and position on the different days of the calendar, and that was the main data astrologers examined to determine omens and portents. The

---

[13] Jean Bottéro, *Mesopotamia: Writing, Reasoning and the Gods*, (Chicago: University of Chicago Press, 1992) pg. 142.
[14] Ibid.

moon, meanwhile, was divided into four quadrants. Each quadrant was associated with a separate section of the Babylonian Empire: the north represented Subartu, the south was Akkad, the east was Elam, and the west was Amurru. The fullness of the moon was significant. Astrologers additionally placed great weight on solstices and eclipses, as well as the different phases of the moon. The size and brightness of the sun and moon were also considered and recorded in clay tablets.

The Deities and Their Planets

Planet	Deity	Deity's Domain
Sun	Shamash	Justice, Truth, and Order
Moon	Sin	Cattle and Fertility
Mercury	Nabu	Wisdom and Writing
Venus	Ishtar	Love, Sexuality, and War
Mars	Nergal	Death, the Underworld, Pestilence, and Plague
Saturn	Ninurta	Healing and Agriculture
Jupiter	Marduk	The City of Babylon

Anyone familiar with the modern zodiac and Greek and Roman mythology will see similarities between the deities the Babylonians assigned to specific planets and their domains, and the ones chosen by the Greeks. These domains also heavily influence how modern astrologers and people interested in astrology in general interpret the presence and movements of different planets. For example, Venus being Ishtar's planet is reminiscent of Venus representing Aphrodite for the Greeks and being a common symbol of love, desire, and sexuality. Likewise, Jupiter is Marduk, who would supplant Anu as the chief Babylonian god once Hammurabi rose to power. In Greek, Jupiter was Zeus, also the chief deity.

Jupiter as Seen by the Cassini Space Probe

The Zodiac

Most information that historians and archaeologists possess about Babylonian astrology comes from a document called MUL.APIN or "The Plow." Dating indicates the tablet was created around 1000 BCE. It contains roughly 71 stars and constellations that the Babylonians observed with some regularity. The Babylonians did keep track of seventeen or eighteen specific constellations but didn't assign them the same meanings that contemporary individuals do. The planetary movement in and around the constellations did have specific meanings that varied based on position. What's interesting about the Babylonian constellations is that they identified most of the major ones associated with the modern zodiac and actually gave them similar names. Some examples are included here:

- Aries: LU.HUN.GA – "Field Worker"
- Taurus: GU.AN.NA – "The Heavenly Bull" or "The Sacred Bull"
- Gemini: MASH.TA.BA – "The Twins"

- Cancer: AL.LUL – "Crayfish"
- Leo: UR.GU.LA – "Lion"
- Virgo: AB.SIN – "The Seed-Furrow" or "Daughter of Sin"
- Libra: ZI.BA.AN.NA or GISH.ERIN – "Heavenly Fate" or "The Scales"
- Scorpio: GIR.TAB – "The Scorpion"
- Sagittarius: PA.BIL.SAG – "The Defender"
- Capricorn: SUHUR.MASH – "The Goat Fish"
- Aquarius: GU.LA – "The Lord of Waters"
- Pisces: SIM.MAH – "Fishes" or "The Tails"

A 15th Century Woodcut of the Zodiac Signs

This image, taken from a European woodcut from the 1400s, demonstrates how Babylonian interpretations of the different constellations, as well as their early work on the zodiac, would go on to influence the Greeks, Romans, and then European culture. This is a little-known fact for many people, but the zodiac was also a popular symbol in Christian artwork, with the image of Jesus often appearing surrounded by the signs of the zodiac. The Babylonians' influence was far-reaching indeed.

Divination

Similar to astrology was the practice of divination. While astrology focused solely on identifying portents in the skies, divination referred to finding signs and omens down on earth in physical mediums regular humans could access. Diviners were the practitioners of this practice, and they relied on many lists of omens similar to astrologers. Some of the mediums they looked at were birds in the sky, the growth of plants, birth defects in humans and animals, and the movement of smoke and water when it was asked questions. Combined with astrology, Babylonian culture dictated that it was possible to figure out what future events pertained to an individual. For example, the Babylonians thought they could tell if someone would live, die, get sick, have a healthy pregnancy, or marry well.

As with astrology, divination included omens, some which were common and some which were never seen. Their lists include some unusual omens with listed meanings—omens that have never appeared in human history. For example, take a cow. It's common for a cow to give birth to a single calf while two is rare. The birth of two calves was a sign or an omen, but the Babylonians didn't stop there. They listed potential outcomes for the births of three, four, five, and even eight calves from a single cow.

Another practice was hepatoscopy. The Babylonians are well-known for their hepatoscopy, which is the examination of the liver of an animal to determine the future. They firmly believed that the liver was the most central and significant organ of human and animal alike. By their logic, the liver was the source of the blood in the body and therefore supplied the life source. A priest, known as a bārû, trained in the practice of hepatoscopy and the interpretation of signs discovered in the liver. Multiple professionals developed a full compendium called the Bārûtu. The Babylonians made clay liver models to better help train bārûs and explain what signs would look like. Archaeologists found several dating to the 19th or 18th century BCE.

The study of the liver could also be done to predict the weather, such as whether there would be favorable conditions for healthy crops. Hepatoscopy was part of the larger practice of studying animal entrails in general for portents, which is called extispicy.

Because the Babylonians had another clear system for determining and predicting the future, divination is also counted as a primitive science for this civilization, even if it was based more in religion and magic than the hard facts common in contemporary study. Similar to astrology, diviners once again based the results of their omens on careful study and then made their own predictions and hypotheses for other results. An individual can also see similarities between the practices of astrology and divination and how the Babylonians studied medicine, seen earlier.

Chapter 4 – Babylonia Before the Babylonians

The Babylonians are frequently understood as another empire in the long history of Mesopotamia that developed from the same peoples that formed earlier civilizations. They are considered broadly Mesopotamian in culture, dress, language, and religion. For this reason, it's important to understand who and what came before the official Babylonian Empire, as the civilization drew heavily from its predecessors such as the Sumerians and Akkadians.

The Origins of Babylonia

The roots of the Babylonians can be traced back to roughly 3500 BCE when a well-developed Sumerian civilization started to emerge. The Sumerians are one of the oldest human civilizations on record. They were followed by a new group of individuals who spoke an early form of Akkadian around 3000 BCE. At some point, these two peoples engaged in such intense trade and social interaction that the majority of the region became bilingual, which allowed for intense and intimate culture sharing and borrowing. Even the languages became mixed together as people started to employ idioms, phrases, words, and even whole portions of grammar to get their ideas across.

Eventually, Akkadian became more popular than the original Sumerian. Some scholars suggest this happened because the number of speakers with Akkadian as a first language slowly started to outnumber those who spoke the original Sumerian, while others believe it's because Akkadian became the language of business and religion. Either way, Mesopotamia saw the decline of significant cities and city-states like the famous Ur, Uruk, Eridu, and Lagash thanks to the rise of the new Akkadian Empire (2334–2154 BCE), which would replace the Sumerian Empire.

However, this doesn't mean that the Sumerians disappeared. Those people were still around and actually became part of the Akkadian Empire. The only thing that changed was that Akkadian language and culture was starting to become more prominent and widespread, similar to how the ancient Roman Empire became Christian, while the people that constituted Sumer and Mesopotamia remained. Even the major religious center of the original Sumerians remained the same; it was just now referred to as Akkadian. This would be the city of Nippur, where residents worshiped the god Enlil. This wouldn't change until Hammurabi emerged as the mighty leader of the Babylonians around the 18th century BCE.

The Sumerians

The Sumerians are the oldest known Mesopotamian civilization and considered to be the first. They settled the region between 5000 and 4500 BCE. Most historians believe they were a western Asian people who moved farther west for greater access to resources and arable land that developed from the deposits of the Tigris and Euphrates Rivers. When in Mesopotamia, they divided into militaristic city-states which traded and fought with one another over territory. The cities were separated from one another by canals, rocky outcrops, and raised terrain that served as protection from attacks. Each city possessed a temple dedicated to a patron god or goddess. The government consisted of a series of powerful, land-owning nobles led either by a religious governor, called an *ensi*, or a king, called a *lugal*.[15]

The Sumerian written history can be dated as far back as the 27th century BCE, although most records come from much later during the 23rd century BCE. This is because around that time, the Sumerians developed a new system of writing based on syllables. Contrary to popular belief, this ancient civilization demonstrated some unusual qualities, such as relative gender equality and cities

---

[15] Harriett Crawford, *Sumer and the Sumerians*, (New York: Cambridge University Press, 2004).

which lacked walls and standing armies. During their early existence, the Sumerians experienced periods of great peace, and royalty and other prominent legislative figures would have both male and female advisors. For the temples, the gender of the high priest would alternate based on the god's form. So, a male god would have a female high priest, and a female god would have a male.

This way of life changed during a span of time called the Early Dynastic Period, which started around 2900 BCE and lasted until c. 2500 BCE. Here, most of the unprotected cities disappeared and society shifted to the governing system mentioned above, where nobles and a high priest or king controlled humans and resources. Women slowly lost their place in society and were confined more and more to a domestic role as agriculture and warfare stripped them of their rights. A great resource for historians about this time period, and one of the oldest pieces of human literature, is the *Epic of Gilgamesh*.[16]

The *Epic of Gilgamesh* was written during the Akkadian Empire, but the man himself was one of the kings of Uruk and the most famous Mesopotamian hero. He ruled at some point between 2800 and 2500 BCE and would eventually be deified, or made a god. His epic provides valuable information about Sumerian values and lifestyles, as well as the influence of religion and the gods on society and culture.

There were a few reasons why the Sumerians slowly faded. One was the natural movement of more ethnic groups and different language-speaking tribes into the region. Another was increased soil salinity, or the presence of rising amounts of salt. This salt made it difficult to grow their staple crop, wheat. Even when farmers switched to barley, which should have been able to tolerate the salinity, it was too late. The Sumerians had to move from their homelands, which upset the balance of power and allowed the Akkadians to gain a regional advantage.

The Akkadians

Originally, the Akkadians were just another group living in Mesopotamia. After the Sumerians struggled and left their homes,

---

16 Stephen Mitchell, *Gilgamesh: A New English Version,* (New York: Free Press, 2004).

the Akkadians managed to gain significant territorial and cultural footholds. Slowly, they built an empire which united the two peoples and brought Akkadian culture to prominence.[17]

The central city of the Akkadian Empire was Akkad, which historians still struggle to precisely locate. Its first powerful ruler was a man named Sargon. His personal background is unknown as he himself made numerous claims, including having a changeling mother and an absent father. Once he aspired to be king, he changed his story so that his mother was actually a high priestess. This would have meant he was a noble and gave him legitimacy to rule. He began his life as a cupbearer to another king and worked his way to being a gardener who cleaned irrigation canals. Here, he formed his first coalition of soldiers from the other workers.

Sargon displaced the original king and then immediately started to expand the Akkadian territory through conquest. He united all of Mesopotamia and then spread across the Euphrates River into an area known as the Levant. Here, he fought and dominated an ancient people known as the Hattians. He replaced any ruler who opposed him with Akkadian nobles and purportedly ruled for 56 years before dying of old age. He expanded trade considerably to include materials like silver and lapis, and spread it north into Assyria, which would become the breadbasket of the Akkadians.

After Sargon's death, the Akkadian Empire remained strong and powerful. The civilization and economy were carefully planned to fully maximize the efficiency of resources and the population. Staple foods like wheat, barley, and oil were kept in massive granaries and measured out to citizens. Taxes could be paid in money, food, or public service—in this way, the Akkadians kept their walls and canals strong through labor. The Akkadian language became ubiquitous throughout the Middle East and spread to nearby territories. Tablets containing it have been found as far as Egypt.[18]

By the 22nd century BCE, though, the Akkadian Empire struggled and toppled after lasting only 180 years. Historians propose a diverse

---

[17] Benjamin R. Foster, *The Age of Agade: Inventing Empire in Ancient Mesopotamia,* (New York: Routledge Publishing, 2016).

[18] Ibid.

array of reasons why this could be as there isn't enough archaeological evidence to indicate a precise cause. The first idea is that there was a massive drought which decimated the empire's agriculture, making their way of life unsustainable. The second is that the empire simply extended itself too far and found itself unable to maintain control over city-states that fought for independence. The third is that nomadic hordes descended upon Mesopotamia and the Akkadian military was not strong enough to stop them. This last theory seems the least likely as the Akkadians held strict control over their immediate territory and there is the least amount of evidence for the nomad hypothesis.

Descendants and successors of the Akkadians possessed their own ideas. According to one preserved tablet, the fall of the empire came about due to the sacrilegious actions of King Naram-Sin, who listened to two lying oracles and sacked a temple protected by the chief god Enlil. As punishment, eight of the gods gathered together and cast down judgment upon the empire. The text reads:

For the first time since cities were built and founded,

The great agricultural tracts produced no grain,

The inundated tracts produced no fish,

The irrigated orchards produced neither syrup nor wine,

The gathered clouds did not rain, the masgurum did not grow.

At that time, one shekel's worth of oil was only one-half quart,

One shekel's worth of grain was only one-half quart…

These sold at such prices in the markets of all the cities!"

He who slept on the roof, died on the roof,

He who slept in the house, had no burial,

People were flailing at themselves from hunger.[19]

As the Akkadian star waned, the Babylonian star rose and would create one of the longest-lasting empires in history.

---

[19] "The Electronic Text Corpus of Sumerian Literature," The University of Oxford, last modified 2004, http://etcsl.orinst.ox.ac.uk/cgi-bin/etcsl.cgi?text=t.2.1.5#

Chapter 5 – The Amorite Dynasty or the First Babylonians

There is little archaeological evidence to indicate when the First Babylonian Dynasty developed since the region possesses a high water table that led to the destruction of old clay materials. The evidence which survives to this day tends to be royal documentation, some literature, and lists of years and their corresponding names. For these reasons, not much is known about the culture and society of the First Babylonians, although historians can clearly trace significant political and cultural events.

The Origins of the Amorite Dynasty

The First Babylonian Dynasty was the Amorite Dynasty, which lasted from 1894-1595 BCE. The Amorites were a semi-nomadic people who lived in Mesopotamia and adopted the Akkadian language while the old Akkadian Empire was still in power. Once the large-scale drought struck the region in the 22nd BCE, the Amorites moved from their lands west of the Euphrates in great numbers and crossed over into more Akkadian territory, where their lifestyle was better suited to the minimal agriculture able to be performed in that region. As the Akkadians and the Assyrians, who still existed in northern Mesopotamia, concentrated on keeping territory close to home, they abandoned the lower section of Mesopotamia. Into this power vacuum came the Amorites, who formed several city-states and small kingdoms.[20]

---

[20] Kemal Yirdirim, *The Ancient Amorites (Amurru) of Mesopotamia,* (LAP Lambert Academic Publishing, 2017).

One of these kingdoms was the small Kazallu, which featured the town of Babylon. Around 1894 BCE, Kazallu started to gain resources and military power. From there, it would gradually conquer the other Amorite kingdoms and unite them to form the first iteration of the Babylonian Empire known as the First Babylonian Dynasty. This dynasty began when a chieftain called Sumu-Abum took the land containing Babylon from Kazallu and attempted to transform it into a minor state. Unfortunately for him, there was a deluge of minor states crammed within the Amorite territory, and he never received recognition or the title of *King of Babylon*. It would seem that the small town simply was not worthy of possessing its own kingship while competing with the others in the area.

Sumu-Abum was succeeded by numerous successors who were additionally unable to acquire the legitimacy of a kingship, not that any of them tried. These three men were Sumu-la-El, Sabium, and Apil-Sin. The next to rule, Sin-Muballit, would be the first Amorite ruler to claim the title *King of Babylon*, but it would seem his regality was only on paper—or clay, as the case may be. The official title only appeared a single time in existing tablets, indicating it was not used frequently. It's unclear whether the town of Babylon remained insignificant due to a lack of ambition or ability on the part of the early Babylonian rulers, or simple overshadowing. After all, Babylon existed in the same region of much older, grander, and more powerful kingdoms like Assyria, Elam, and Larsa.

Hammurabi

Soon, though, Babylon would become grand with the reign of its sixth ruler, the legendary and eminent Hammurabi.

Hammurabi, also referred to as Hammurapi in some ancient texts, lived from c.1810-c.1750 BCE and reigned from 1792-1750 BCE. He came to power at the tender age of eighteen following the abdication of his father, who was ill and feared his death approached. Hammurabi is simultaneously remembered as a dynamic, efficient conqueror and the creator of one of the oldest and most detailed law codes of the ancient world, which was inscribed on a massive black stele. During his reign, he experienced immense success and conquered many of the other kingdoms of Mesopotamia and the surrounding area, including the tough Elam, Larsa, Mari, and

Eshnunna.[21]

Upon ascending to the throne, Hammurabi's first actions were to improve the structure of Babylon, reform the army, and establish a bureaucracy with clear policies for taxation to bolster military and royal spending. The government relied less on the power of additional nobles and became more centralized, with a system of scribes and administrators who could carry out official business with minimum disruptions. Hammurabi and his generals disciplined the army and ensured it was equipped with the best equipment available, which meant improved bronze weapons, leather armor and boots, shields, helmets, and chariots.

Hammurabi received some help in this regard. Before leaving the throne, Sin-Muballit, Hammurabi's father, had begun a system of expansion into the neighboring kingdoms and attempted to assert Babylonian hegemony throughout southern Mesopotamia. His dreams were thwarted, however, by the presence of dominant kingdoms to the north. Hammurabi, therefore, came to power in a precarious and complex geopolitical situation. Elam to the east frequently attempted to exact tribute from the minor southern Mesopotamian kingdoms like Babylon, and the Assyrians to the north controlled the largest extent of territory and possessed a well-developed and expansive culture. One of Hammurabi's strokes of luck would be the sudden death of the Assyrian king, which left the territory in poorly protected fragments.[22]

But for the first few decades of his reign, Hammurabi had little to do with the affairs of other states. Instead, he focused on building his own kingdom. It wasn't until Elam launched an invasion of southern Mesopotamia and destroyed the kingdom of Eshnunna that Babylon responded to external stimuli. After taking Eshnunna, the king of Elam wished to consolidate his power. To do so, he attempted to start a war between Babylon and Larsa. Upon discovering the duplicity, Hammurabi struck a deal with the ruler of Larsa, turned around, and crushed the Elamites. The Babylonians contributed the majority of the military might.

---

[21] Marc Van De Mieroop, *King Hammurabi of Babylon: A Biography,* (Malden: Blackwell Publishing, 2005).

[22] Ibid.

Hammurabi next began a protracted war with the Assyrian Empire to the north where most of his troops were concentrated. He sought to control Mesopotamia and gain some form of dominance in the region, especially since Assyria ruled over the Hurrians and Hattians, the northeast Levant, and central Mesopotamia. Taking the territory would contribute to the resources of Babylon as well as provide access to arable agricultural land and new trade routes. Hammurabi would struggle for decades with two separate kings: Shamshi-Adad I and Ishme-Dagan, named after an influential deity.[23] Eventually, Babylon gained the upper hand, and the new king of Assyria, Mut-Askur, was forced to pay tribute to Babylon by handing over Assyria's colonies near Anatolia. The below map shows Assyria's location in respect to Babylon, which occupied parts of the Akkadian and Sumerian territories.

While asserting dominance over the Assyrians, Hammurabi completed his famous law code, which drew heavily from previous sources created in Sumer, Akkad, and Assyria itself. Its creation began shortly after the expulsion of the Elamites and would take several years to complete. The Code of Hammurabi contains roughly

23 Ibid.

282 laws dictating the proper punishments and courses of action for a variety of crimes, including murder, theft, adultery, and improper medical practices. Punishments were harsh and draconian, frequently involving mutilation or death for the guilty party. Accusing someone of a crime of which they were innocent resulted in the death of the accuser. Some memorable laws include:

2 – "If any one bring an accusation against a man, and the accused go to the river and leap into the river, if he sink in the river his accuser shall take possession of his house. But if the river prove that the accused is not guilty, and he escape unhurt, then he who had brought the accusation shall be put to death, while he who leaped into the river shall take possession of the house that had belonged to his accuser."

25 – "If fire break out in a house, and someone who comes to put it out cast his eye upon the property of the owner of the house, and take the property of the master of the house, he shall be thrown into that self-same fire."

130 – "If a man violate the wife (betrothed or child-wife) of another man, who has never known a man, and still lives in her father's house, and sleep with her and be surprised, this man shall be put to death, but the wife is blameless."

141 – "If a man's wife, who lives in his house, wishes to leave it, plunges into debt, tries to ruin her house, neglects her husband, and is judicially convicted: if her husband offer her release, she may go on her way, and he gives her nothing as a gift of release. If her husband does not wish to release her, and if he take another wife, she shall remain as servant in her husband's house."

195 – "If a son strike his father, his hands shall be hewn off."

196 – "If a man put out the eye of another man, his eye shall be put out."[24]

Cultural Changes and Decline

The rise of the Babylonians resulted in major cultural shifts. One of the most significant was the transition of major cities. Before

---

[24] "The Code of Hammurabi," The Avalon Project, Yale Law School, last modified 2017, http://avalon.law.yale.edu/ancient/hamframe.asp.

Hammurabi, the most important Mesopotamian city was Nippur, where the patron god was Enlil, the chief deity in the pantheon. With Hammurabi, the focus was shifted to the city of Babylon and the new chief deity was Marduk, who originated in southern Mesopotamia. The only exception to this rule was in certain segments of the old Assyria, where Ashur and Ishtar remained more influential. Literacy additionally improved among the upper classes, and the number of scribes increased. The size and population of Babylon and southern Mesopotamia in general exploded, and numerous palaces, temples, and bas-reliefs were created to display the area's newfound prominence.

Following Hammurabi's death, the situation deteriorated rapidly. The problem with southern Mesopotamia was that there were no geographic boundaries that provided significant protection from invaders. Hammurabi was replaced by a relatively ineffectual leader, one Samsu-iluna, who lost the tip of southern Mesopotamia to an Akkadian-speaking king. This territory would not be reunited with the rest of Babylon for 272 years and became the Sealand Dynasty. Next, the Assyrians to the north pushed back against the Babylonians and reclaimed territory after six years of warfare. Although several rulers fought to regain the Sealand Dynasty and sections of Assyria, they failed. Two more kings focused on building projects instead.

The final Amorite ruler of Babylon would be Samsu-Ditana, who struggled against the Kassites.[25] The Kassites were an unusual group which spoke an isolated language and hailed from contemporary northwest Iran. They chipped away at Babylonian power and were then followed by the Hittites around 1595 BCE. These Hittites sacked Babylon and left the region, leaving a destroyed city ripe for the taking by the Kassites. Historians are unsure of the exact year of the sack of Babylon but give three dates: 1499 BCE, 1531 BCE, and 1595 BCE.

---

[25] Yildirim, *The Ancient Amorites.*

Chapter 6 – The First Fall of Babylon and the Rise of the Kassites

Gandash of Mari founded the Kassite Dynasty in Mesopotamia and potentially led the invasion of Babylon, although sources are unclear. Similar to the Amorites, the Kassites were not native to Mesopotamia and instead migrated from the Zagros mountain range in northwestern Iran. There doesn't remain any genetic evidence for scientists to figure out the exact ethnic affiliation of the Kassites, but they did not belong to the same general language group of the Babylonians or any of the other civilizations in Mesopotamia or the nearby Levant. It's entirely possible the Kassites were an isolated people, although some suspect they were actually Indo-European and speaking a dialect which had morphed from little interaction with others.[26]

The Kassites would possess the longest dynasty to ever exist in Babylonia. They renamed the city Karduniaš and made several changes to the general role of the monarchy. Previously, the king was seen as a divine figure and could be deified. None of the Kassite rulers ever included any divine attributes in their personal descriptions and separated themselves from the general idea that to be king was a holy office. None of them ever added the word for "god" to their names either, which had been a common practice

---

[26] L.W. King, *Chronicles concerning early Babylonian kings: including records of the early history of the Kassites and the country of the sea*, (London: Luzac and co., 2014).

throughout Mesopotamia. Despite these changes though, Babylon would remain one of the holiest cities of the region and the priests of the Mesopotamian religion retained their power. The pantheon stayed relatively unchanged.

Indeed, the Kassites changed little. Their only major contributions were the incorporation of the Kassite language, although many switched to Akkadian; the retention of a tribal structure rather than small family units; and the artistic addition of special carved stones called kudurrus, which were used as boundary markers throughout the empire.

The Kassites proved to be weak monarchs. Although they managed to push into Babylonian territory, they didn't make it farther for over a century. Instead, the kings focused for a long time on maintaining peaceful relations with their neighbors. After Gandash of Mari came Agum II, who ascended to the throne in 1595 BCE. His territory extended southward from the midpoint of the Euphrates River to modern-day Iran, and Agum II realized it would be difficult to manage such a large swathe of land if he went to war with his neighbors. Instead, he maintained peaceful relationships with the closest powers, including the king of Assyria to the north. The only people he fought were the Hittites, who still wanted to claim some Babylonian territory after sacking the city. During his reign, he proclaimed that Marduk, Babylon's patron deity, was equal to the Kassite Shuqamuna.[27]

Agum II's successors likewise kept to themselves and focused on making Babylon a cohesive territorial state rather than a series of powerful cities. While frequently overshadowed by larger neighbors like Elam and Assyria, Babylon established significant trade routes and conducted successful diplomacy through marriage treaties with Assyria. Foreign merchants and traders flocked to Babylon to exchange goods, and the Kassites started sending their own merchants and traders as far as Egypt to acquire luxuries like Nubian gold. After building the state into a stable empire, the Kassites started to push southward to reclaim the tip of Mesopotamia claimed by the Sealand Dynasty. They would succeed and welcome it back into the empire.

[27] Ibid.

To maintain control over their territory, the Kassites divided the empire into smaller provinces overseen by an influential governor loyal to the crown. They also established two royal cities, keeping Babylon as one and designating Dur-Kurigalzu as the other. Provincial centers became major trade centers and sources of culture even though the Kassites themselves failed to spread literacy and literature during their reign. Temples and important buildings were torn down or meticulously updated and rebuilt to further cement the significance of the cities.

Everything seemed to go well for the Kassites until relations with Assyria deteriorated. In the mid-15th century BCE, Kurigalzu I and Ashur-bel-nisheshu signed a treaty to facilitate peace and trade, but the next few centuries were spent struggling for dominion in Mesopotamia. Problems escalated when Ashur-uballit I ascended to the Assyrian throne in 1365 BCE and solicited aid from the Hittites and Egyptians to become the greatest power in the region. Ashur-uballit I sacked Babylon after his daughter's husband, the king of the Kassites, was found murdered. To avenge his son-in-law, he deposed the new monarch and chose a new ruler from the Kassite line.

Further attacks would come from the following rulers of Assyria for various reasons. Some, like Enlil-nirari (1330-1319 BCE) sought to expand into Babylonian territory and succeeded in annexing chunks to assimilate into the Assyrian Empire. Others desired full conquest, and Tukulti-Ninurta I (1244-1208 BCE) even succeeded and ruled the entirety of Babylon for eight years from the city itself. He would be the first king of Babylon to be ethnically Mesopotamian, as the Amorites and Kassites were all outsiders.

Eventually, an Assyrian governor took over the throne for the monarchy, and the royal generals were able to return to the main section of Assyria rather than remain and rule. A string of governors would rule for Babylonia in their stead until Adad-shuma-usur (1216-1189 BCE) decided late in his reign to separate from Assyria and once again attempt to form an independent Babylonian empire. He struggled with the king, Enlil-kudurri-usur, until his death, and a civil war continued afterward. Slowly, Babylonia shrugged off the shackles of Assyria, and the Kassites formed a semi-independent empire once more.[28]

Meli-Shipak II followed and held a peaceful reign by losing no territory and not suffering from the Late Bronze Age collapse that decimated the powers in the Levant, the kingdom of Canaan, and the Egyptian Empire to the west. The next two kings were not as lucky and experienced protracted warfare with the Assyrians, who resumed their expansionist policies and attempted to take northern Babylonia between 1171 and 1155 BCE. Then Elam attacked, taking most of eastern Babylonia and incorporating it into their kingdom. In 1155 BCE, the Kassite Dynasty fell once the Assyrians and Elamites succeeded in tearing apart Babylon, sacking the city, and murdering the final Kassite king.

Dynasty IV of Babylonia

The next ruler of Babylonia would then be the Elamites. They did not keep the territory long as their expansionist tendencies brought them head to head with the equally voracious Assyrians, who wished to claim the entirety of Mesopotamia for themselves. Elam and Assyria entered a brutal war which resulted in an Elamite loss, an Assyrian victory, and the creation of a new Mesopotamian dynasty in Babylon. The first ruler would be Marduk-kabit-ahheshu, who ruled from 1155-1139 BCE. He was the second native Mesopotamian to hold the throne and would establish Dynasty IV of Babylon, which lasted 125 years. Although hailing from Assyria, Marduk-kabit-ahheshu eventually warred with the Assyrian monarchy over border territory. Although he captured the southern city of Ekallatum, he lost it and would be defeated by King Ashur-Dan I.

The next two kings also tried to conquer sections of Assyria but failed and were forced to sign unfavorable treaties that cost Babylon land and resources. Then, another successful monarch came, one who is well-known to contemporary audiences: Nebuchadnezzar I (1124-1103 BCE).

Nebuchadnezzar I was the most successful ruler of Dynasty IV. Unlike his predecessors, he possessed advanced knowledge of military strategy and conquest and succeeded in defeating the

---

[28] Ibid.

Elamites and driving them out of Babylon. He went so far as to follow the soldiers into Elam itself, captured the capital of Susa, and returned several sacred Babylonian artifacts stolen during previous conquests to Babylon. Elam would then disintegrate after the assassination of its king, fully eliminating the state as a threat during Nebuchadnezzar I's life.

Afterward, Nebuchadnezzar I attempted to expand into Assyrian territory, namely the regions of Aram and Anatolia. However, he was unsuccessful and chose to instead devote his time to once against bolstering and beautifying Babylon in his old age. While doing this, he shored up the empire's defenses, especially against the Assyrians and Arameans, which were another group slowly rising on the corpses of their neighbors. After he died, his two sons messed up his successes. The first lost small sections of Babylonian territory to Assyria, but the second truly failed by declaring a full war and losing catastrophically to the king of the time, one Tiglath-Pileser I (1115-1076 BCE).[29]

Tiglath-Pileser I annexed massive swathes of land, expanding his own empire while significantly weakening the Babylonians. Then, famine struck. The population of Babylon starved, and the military became weakened from a lack of food and resources. Like vultures preying on a dying animal, the peoples of the Levant swooped down upon Babylon and attempted to pick the territory clean of any remaining valuables and resources. The kings were powerless to stop the onslaught from the Semitic Aramaeans and Suteans from the Levant. At the same time, relations with Assyria soured further to the point where Assyria invaded, deposed the king, and made Babylon a vassal. It wasn't until the Middle Assyrian Empire descended into a costly civil war that the Babylonians were able to escape vassalage and regain independence once more.

In true fashion, they were not left alone. From the west came new groups of Semitic-speaking peoples who sought to migrate from the Levant following the havoc and chaos caused by the Bronze Age collapse, or the breakdown of civilization due to a combination of environmental and military factors. These peoples tended to be

---

[29] A. Kirk Grayson, *Assyrian Rulers of the Early First Millennium BCE (1114-859 BC)*, (Toronto: University of Toronto Press, 1991).

Arameans and Suteans, who took over huge sections of the Babylonian countryside and refused to leave.

A Century of Chaos, 1026–911 BCE

Aramean marauders managed to depose the ruling Babylonian dynasty around 1026 BCE, which plunged the capital city into chaos. Anarchy ruled for twenty years, during which time there was no monarch on the throne. Eventually, a new dynasty developed in southern Mesopotamia, around the location of the old Sealand Dynasty, which had been incorporated into Babylon once more by the Kassites. This new dynasty, referred to as Dynasty V, only lasted from 1025-1004 BCE but managed to eliminate some of the chaos in the empire. Babylon still ended up losing northern territory to the Assyrians, including the city of Atila.

Several more short dynasties would follow, one ruled by the Kassites and another by the leftover Amorites. They fell quickly, and the Arameans once again savaged the countryside and raised anarchy in the cities. Again, two short dynasties appeared, bringing Babylon up to Dynasty IX with King Ninurta-kudurri-usur II. Although weak and struck with hordes of Arameans and Suteans, Babylon once again had someone seated squarely on the throne. Even more territory wound up in the hands of the Assyrians and Elamites.

Chapter 7 – Assyrian Domination and Rule, 911-619 BCE

Babylonia suffered throughout the remainder of the 10th century BCE as chaos was the name of the game. The government could not reorganize, and resources became scarce. Further migrations of nomads made it difficult for the population to sustain itself. Some of the new arrivals were the Chaldeans, who entered in the southeast and set up permanent settlements. This group was another Semitic-language speaking culture that added and contributed heavily to the overall Babylonian society. By 850 BCE, the Chaldeans established their own land in Babylonian territory and started to send their culture north through natural migration, trade, and human interaction.

Aside from roaming migratory groups, Babylonia faced additional struggles through the formation of the Neo-Assyrian Empire in 911 BCE. The Neo-Assyrian Empire was not only the largest Mesopotamian empire to date but also the most massive in the history of the world. It would conquer much of the known world in Mesopotamia, the Levant, and other sections of northeastern Africa and western Asia. Among its territories were Babylonia itself, Persia, Israel, Judah, sections of Egypt, and the burgeoning Arabia states. This map demonstrates its extent:

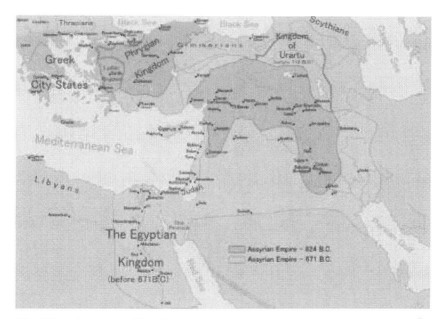

The Neo-Assyrian Empire

The empire's founder was a man named Adad-nirari II. He entered Babylonia and conquered huge sections of it, eventually forcing the entire region under its control. He started by attacking and defeating one of Babylonia's leaders, Shamash-mudammiq, and took land north of the Diyala River and several important towns around the middle of Mesopotamia. He continued his push forward when a new leader took control, this time Nabu-shuma-ukin I. The successors of Shamash-mudammiq, Tukulti-Ninurta II and Ashurnasirpal II, consolidated their hold over Babylonia and officially forced it to become a vassal of the much greater Neo-Assyrian Empire. This meant it now needed to pay tribute and essentially give up military or economic resources as the Assyrians demanded.

After Ashurnasirpal II, the next Assyrian leader—Shalmaneser III—managed to sack the city of Babylon, kill the Babylonian king, and take control of the invasive migratory tribes that dominated southern Babylonia, including the Chaldeans. The rulers of Babylonia would remain vassals until 780 BCE. Then, the foreign Marduk-apla-usur took advantage of a civil war in Assyria and ascended to the Babylonian throne. He was a Chaldean and quickly drew the ire of the Assyrian rulers, who were not happy with his usurpation. The Assyrian king came down, retook northern Babylonia, and then made Marduk-apla-usur sign a new border treaty that gave Assyria more territory. However, Marduk-apla-usur was allowed to remain on the throne and ruled until 769 BCE. Another Chaldean took the throne, and then another.[30]

Another Babylonian would not retake the throne until 748 BCE, when Nabonassar overthrew the Chaldeans, stabilized Babylonia under his rule, and retained good relations with Assyria. He kept the peace for three years until a new Assyrian king came to power and once again tried to conquer Babylonia. This leader, Tiglath-Pileser III, sacked Babylon—again—and remade Babylonia into a vassal state. This situation continued until 729 BCE when the Assyrian royal line decided to just incorporate Babylonia into its empire instead of relying on the vassalage of Babylonian kings, who were clearly untrustworthy and bad at their jobs.

Around this time, Babylonian Akkadian stopped being the main language as the Assyrians started to insert their own language. This was Eastern Aramaic, which possessed a couple of linguistic differences. Assyrian culture additionally weaved its way throughout Mesopotamia, displacing many original practices. These changes would continue even as revolts started to form throughout former Babylonia.

A Chaldean chieftain south of Babylon by the name of Marduk-apla-iddina II fomented unrest and revolt, and gained immense support not only from other Chaldeans but from the Elamites to the east. This new power-hungry individual managed to gain the throne in Babylon and ruled between 721 and 710 BCE. The main reason for his success was that the Assyrian king, Sargon II, was busy attempting to put down two groups known as the Cimmerians and the Scythians, who had attacked Assyrian vassals outside of Mesopotamia. When the king is away, it's time for the usurpers to play, after all.

Unfortunately for this usurper, the king came back. Sargon II defeated Marduk-apla-iddina II and threw him out of the palace. Marduk-apla-iddina II fled to Elam, where he lived with some of his former allies and protectors. Sargon II became the new king of

---

[30] Trevor Bryce, *Babylonia: A Very Short Introduction* (Oxford: Oxford University Press, 2016).

Babylon.[31]

Sargon II remained a successful and efficient ruler until he was killed in battle around 705 BCE. His soldiers were unable to recover his body, and authority and the throne went to his son, Sennacherib. After a few years of direct ruling, Sennacherib decided to pass the Babylonian throne to his own son so he could focus more on conquest and the rest of the Neo-Assyrian Empire. Strife and warfare soon came to Babylon again as the Elamites tried to take the territory once more. One Elamite, Nergal-ushezib, killed the Assyrian prince in Babylon and gained power, which led to Sennacherib returning, beating back Elam, and sacking the city of Babylon once again, effectively destroying the city. The population was no doubt thrilled to be sacked yet another time, but no sources remain to give a commoner's perspective on the constant political turmoil and warfare.

This could have been the end, but in true historical fashion, it was not. Sennacherib's other sons chose to murder their father while he was praying at a temple in Nineveh in 681 BCE, leaving a power vacuum. The new Assyrian king placed a puppet leader on the Babylonian throne when who should return but Marduk-apla-iddina II. He deposed the puppet king and took power once more, only to be thoroughly thrashed by Esarhaddon. Marduk-apla-iddina II once more fled to Elam with his tail between his legs, where he would eventually die as an exile.

The Assyrian king Esarhaddon was potentially the best thing to happen to the city of Babylon around this time. After defeating Marduk-apla-iddina II, he returned to Babylon and ruled it personally, choosing to rebuild the city and focus on peace instead of expansion. Upon his death, he kept the Neo-Assyrian Empire together but requested that his eldest son rule in Babylon and his youngest son, the famous Ashurbanipal, rule as the more influential king of Assyria.[32]

Anyone who knows anything about brothers will see how this decision fared. The oldest son, Shamash-shum-ukin, spent decades as the subject of Ashurbanipal and finally got fed up with the

[31] Ibid.
[32] Ibid.

situation. He publicly declared that Babylon, not Nineveh, should be the capital of the empire, developed a military, and set out to revolt against Ashurbanipal. He combined the forces of almost everyone who resented Assyrian rule and subjugation, including the Babylonians themselves, the Persians, Elamites, Chaldeans, Medes, the Arameans, and others. Unfortunately for Shamash-shum-ukin, Ashurbanipal was both a scholar and a skilled strategist. He thoroughly routed and decimated his brother's forces, sacking Babylon once again, destroying Elam, and subjugating all of the peoples who opposed him through violence, brutality, and savagery. Lucky for Shamash-shum-ukin, the older brother died in battle and did not live to see his little brother's wrath. A new governor named Kandalanu was given Babylon to rule.

Was it time for peace now? No.

Like all mortals, Ashurbanipal died. His son, Ashur-etil-ilani, took the throne following Ashurbanipal's passing in 627 BCE and tried to be a successful ruler, but the Neo-Assyrian Empire became the scene of convoluted and savage civil wars as Ashurbanipal's generals and other nobles tried to wrest power from the young king. Some historians believe these battles were exacerbated by poor environmental conditions that resulted in a severe drought and limited resources.[33] Ashur-etil-ilani was betrayed by his own military commander, who was ousted after only a year by another man. This one, Sinsharishkun, ruled between 622 and 612 BCE before succumbing to the ravages of ongoing civil conflict.

During all of this turmoil, Babylonia took the opportunity to free itself. A Chaldean called Nabopolassar organized a large-scale rebellion and revolt, eventually liberating the region and ending the centuries of tribute and vassalage that characterized Babylonia under the Assyrians.

---

[33] Adam W. Schneider and Selim F. Adali, ""No harvest was reaped:" demographic and climate factors in the decline of the Neo-Assyrian Empire," *Climate Change* 127, no. 3 (2014): 435-446.

Chapter 8 – The Neo-Babylonian Empire

Babylonia's Assyrian problems weren't over, but the time of Assyrian control had come to an end. Soon, the Neo-Assyrian Empire would be replaced with the Neo-Babylonian as the Babylonians discovered their new position of power over Mesopotamia. The journey to a new empire began with the Chaldean Nabopolassar, who set the stage for an independent Babylonian state.[34] He would be the founder of a new dynasty called Dynasty XI, which would survive until roughly 539 BCE. It consisted of six rulers:

- Nabopolassar from 626-605 BCE
- Nabu-kudurri-usur II (Nebuchadnezzar II) from 605-562 BCE
- Amel-Marduk from 562-560 BCE
- Neriglissar from 560-556 BCE
- Labasi-Marduk in 556 BCE only
- Nabonidus from 556-539 BCE

These kings would control the Neo-Babylonian Empire for almost a century. Without their work, Babylonia would have been unable to escape further domination by outside forces, especially as more and more ethnic groups and tribes struggled to control the same amount

---

[34] Bryce, *Babylonia*.

of territory. The Neo-Babylonian Empire represented a unique golden age for Babylonia before it finally descended once more into vassalage and obscurity from the sheer pressure of all of these outside forces, as well as from the rise of a new threat.

But before the shadow of a rival empire arrived, the story began with Nabopolassar.

Nabopolassar

Nabopolassar managed to sit on the throne in Babylon undisturbed for three years while bloody civil wars raged in Assyria. Eventually, though, a claimant to the throne consolidated his power and set his sights once more on southern Mesopotamia. This would be Sin-shar-ishkun, who had murdered his brother in battle, seized the Assyrian throne, and focused on the conquest of Babylonia once more. Nabopolassar was not an unseasoned warrior and had been expecting Assyrian resistance to Babylonian independence. Although Assyrian forces camped along the borders of Babylonia for seven years, Nabopolassar resisted invasion. He admittedly was aided by the fact that the Assyrian civil wars raged on, frequently distracting his enemy.

Nabopolassar additionally made headway into Assyria itself, capturing the influential city of Nippur in 619 BCE. Nippur was a part of Babylonia but had been one of the centers of pro-Assyrian sentiment, meaning its conquest was a significant political maneuver for the would-be king of a new Babylonia. Nabopolassar continued to consolidate his hold of southern Mesopotamia and watched as the other Assyrian colonies slowly started to free themselves from vassalage and servitude.

The Ruins of Nippur in Modern Iraq

Around 616 BCE, Nabopolassar tried to take territory from the remnants of the Neo-Assyrian Empire. He besieged the cities of Arrapha and Assur, but Sin-shar-ishkun expected the attack and forced the Babylonians back to their own lands. Here, the two forces stayed at an impasse. Neither Assyria nor Babylonia possessed any power to eliminate the other, forcing them to become disgruntled neighbors.

The impasse ended when a former vassal of the Assyrians, a leader named Cyaxares, attacked Sin-shar-ishkun. Cyaxares ruled over several different Iranian ethnic groups such as the Parthians, Medes, and Persians. He attacked in 615 BCE, sacked Arrapha, destroyed Kalhu—also called Nimrud in contemporary sources—and then formed an alliance with the Cimmerians and Scythians. Together, the three forces besieged and conquered Assur. Nabopolassar and the Babylonians were uninvolved but still benefited greatly from the destruction of Assyrian power. Nabopolassar chose to form alliances with these new powers, signing treaties with the Medes, Scythians, Persians, Cimmerians, and other Iranian peoples.

Around 613 BCE, the Assyrians rallied themselves and managed to repel the concerted efforts of the Babylonians and their new allies. This led to Nabopolassar combining his forces with Cyaxares to create one large army consisting of over six different cultural tribes/groups. Together, the sextuplet converged on the Assyrian capital of Nineveh. The sheer size of the army proved to be too gargantuan for the weakened Assyrians to handle, and the city walls crumbled following a three-month siege. Then, the fighting continued on a smaller scale, with forces fighting house by house within the massive city. Soon, Sin-shar-ishkun died defending the city.[35]

Sources get a bit murky about what happened next. A series of tablets known as the Babylonian Chronicles indicate that an Assyrian general briefly became king and was offered the chance to become a vassal to the coalition besieging Nineveh. By all accounts, the general refused, fought his way out of the city, and created a new capital in the city of Harran. Here, he managed to maintain a base of power for five years before Harran was lost in 608 BCE. With the majority of the Assyrian forces destroyed, it was time to turn Babylonian attention to the Egyptians.

Pharaoh Necho II became involved in the war in Mesopotamia around 609 BCE. The Egyptians were one of the vassals of Assyria and attempted to aid their former commanders, but found themselves slowly outnumbered even though they brought Greek mercenaries and were joined by what remained of the Assyrian military. Babylonia, still led by Nabopolassar, spent years trying to drive the Egyptians back, aided by their new allies from Syria, Israel, and a few places in Arabia and Asia Minor. Aiding Nabopolassar was his son, Nebuchadnezzar II (Nabu-kudurri-usur II), who was one of the best military commanders seen in Babylonia in years.

The war between the former Assyrian vassals and Egyptians culminated in the Battle of Carchemish in 605 BCE. There aren't good records of this battle as the most complete source of information comes from a tablet known as the Nebuchadnezzar Chronicle, which naturally praises the Babylonian commander and claims he had a decisive victory. Historians do know that the former Assyrian vassals went into battle with 18,000 total troops while the Egyptians had 40,000. Through superior military strategy and taking advantage of natural resources, Nebuchadnezzar II routed the Egyptian army, inflicting maximum damages while taking minimal losses.

---

[35] Ibid.

Nebuchadnezzar II

The Neo-Assyrian domination was no more. Northern Mesopotamia largely went to the Medes, while the Babylonians focused on rebuilding their territory in the south. Nabopolassar died in 605 BCE, and Nebuchadnezzar II became king in his stead. Nebuchadnezzar II experienced one of the longest reigns of any Babylonian king and became well known for his building projects throughout the empire. He rebuilt all of the empire's ruined, sacked, and destroyed cities, redesigning them and constructing on a truly extravagant scale with new walls, temples, and works of art.[36]

Babylon became a city of legend—beautiful, immense, spectacular, and characterized by unusual and delightful architecture. Babylon stretched over three square miles in length, which was no easy feat during the Iron Age. Nebuchadnezzar II gave it double walls to keep out invaders—potentially because of all of the sacking—and built deep moats for added protection. The Euphrates River appears to have gone through the center of the city, providing aesthetic beauty but also the practicalities of a nearby trade route and fresh water. In the center of the center, he placed a ziggurat known as Etemenanki near the Temple of Marduk, the city's patron god. Historians believe that Etemenanki was the inspiration for the Tower of Babel of legend.

---

[36] Ibid.

The Tower of Babel by Pieter Bruegel the Elder, 1563

The ruins of the Babylon that Nebuchadnezzar II built remain the single largest archaeological site in the Middle East. They spread out over 2,000 acres of land and include great remains such as the Ishtar Gate and the Processional Way. The Ishtar Gate was an extremely lavish entryway into the city of Babylon and was built as the eighth gate into the inner city. It was dedicated to the goddess Ishtar.

Aside from being focused on domestic development, Nebuchadnezzar II continued his work as a successful military commander. He invaded Syria and Phoenicia and forced several major cities and territories to become Babylonian vassals, including Tyre and Damascus. He also went to Asia Minor and started to build up colonies there to receive a steady supply of tribute and resources. The Neo-Babylonian Empire became like the Neo-Assyrians, forced to campaign every year just to maintain its territory. If Nebuchadnezzar II did not, the vassals would revolt.[37]

Around 601 BCE, Nebuchadnezzar II once again butted heads with the Egyptians and then moved on to conquer parts of Arabia and then captured Jerusalem in 597. However, the Egyptians soon

---

[37] Josette Elayi, *The History of Phoenicia*, (Lockwood Press, 2018).

marched in during an attempt to regain control in the Near East. The Babylonians briefly became occupied with trying to fend off the hordes of the latest pharaoh, and Judah took the opportunity to revolt and try to reestablish its independence. Nebuchadnezzar II came right back, captured Jerusalem in 587 BCE, destroyed the famous Solomon's Temple, deported thousands of Jewish people to Babylon, and burned the city to the ground. Even though he had good qualities, Nebuchadnezzar II was nothing if not brutal to his enemies.

A decade before his death, Nebuchadnezzar II had extended the Neo-Babylonian Empire to its greatest extent. Territory covered not only Babylonia, but also Assyria, Israel, northern Arabia, a good chunk of Asia Minor, Phoenicia, and Philistia. He even invaded Egypt in 568 BCE but was not successful.

The Other Four Kings of Dynasty XI

The remaining four rulers of the Neo-Babylonian Empire were not as successful as the first two. When Nebuchadnezzar II perished in 562 BCE, he was replaced by his son, Amel-Marduk. He did not rule long as his brother-in-law, Neriglissar, appears to have murdered him and taken his place in 560 BCE. Why? Some think that Amel-Marduk was ineffective and attempted to remove his father's policies concerning territories and vassal states, which didn't go over well. By all accounts, Neriglissar was a reasonable and stable ruler who continued the trend of public works during the brief four years he was in power. He set about restoring some of the older temples and successfully defeated the powers of Cilicia in Asia Minor.[38]

Neriglissar died young in 556 BCE, and power passed to his son, who was only a child. It took nine months for a conspiracy emerged to murder the boy, Labashi-Marduk. The conspirators then named a man called Nabonidus as the new king. He would be the last ruler, and most believe he was not an ethnic Babylonian or Chaldean but actually an Assyrian from Harran. He even described himself as coming from unimportant and insignificant stock, although his mother appeared to have been a priestess or servant at the temple of a moon god while his father was a commoner.

---

[38] Ibid.

Although Nabonidus was a great soldier, he had no sense when it came to administration and frequently left his son in charge of the kingdom. To make matters worse, he became hated because he tried to suppress the worship of Marduk, the patron god of Babylon, and instead wanted to elevate the worshipers of Sin, the Assyrian moon god. Nabonidus' end would come at the hands of the Persians, who were growing in strength in the east and forming a powerful empire under Cyrus the Great, who had numerous supporters in Babylon itself.

Chapter 9 – The Persian Conquest and Hellenistic Period

Babylonia might not have fallen if Nabonidus had been a better ruler, but the odds were stacked against him. The population repeatedly expressed its dissatisfaction with his new social and cultural policies, but he didn't listen. He continued to elevate the status of the cult of Sin while pushing back Marduk. When he did decide to focus on Marduk instead, he attempted to centralize worship at the temple in Babylon itself, which alienated the local priesthoods that dotted the landscape of the Neo-Babylonian Empire. Nabonidus' own military hated him as well because he spent his time focusing on rebuilding the towns, unearthing old excavation records, and generally acting like a modern historian or archaeologist rather than as a warrior king.[39]

Nabonidus attempted to pacify the military by placing the defense of the empire in the hands of one of his favorite soldiers, Belshazzar. Although Belshazzar was an exceptional soldier, he was a terrible diplomat that managed to make the Babylonian elites hate him in record time. In particular, Belshazzar seemed to have concentrated military forces in Assyria rather than in southern Mesopotamia, which would leave Babylon open to attack and keep the military away from home for long periods of time without conquest. The fact that both men were also Assyrian rather than Babylonian or Chaldean further incensed the nobility.

---

[39] Ibid.

The Rise of Cyrus the Great

The Neo-Babylonian Empire's greatest enemy would appear in the form of Cyrus the Great.[40] Around 550 BCE, he was the Achaemenid Persian king of a city in Elam who led a revolt against his superior, Astyages. Astyages was the king of Medes who kept the Median Empire together to the east of Babylonia. The Median Empire was the term for the civilization created by the Medes, whom readers will recognize as one of the Babylonian allies against Assyria. They dominated the other native Iranian peoples that lived in the region of modern-day Iran. Cyrus the Great convinced the army of Astyages to betray him, and Cyrus then established himself as a new powerful leader in Ecbatana. His revolt ended the Median Empire and pushed the Persians to the top of the hierarchy of the numerous Iranian peoples living in the region. Within three years, Cyrus was the king of Persia proper, crushing Assyrian revolts and making preparations to enter the Neo-Babylonian Empire for conquest.

---

[40] Cameron Shamsabad, *History's Forgotten Father: Cyrus the Great,* (Shamsabad Publishing, 2014).

The Four-Winged Representation of Cyrus the Great

After spending eleven years consolidating his rule, Cyrus turned his attention to the Neo-Babylonian Empire. In 539 BCE, he invaded. Here is where the source material becomes murky once more. Primary sources such as the Babylonian Chronicles and an artifact called the Cyrus Cylinder—literally an ancient cylinder with writing engraved in the pottery—indicate that the city of Babylon fell to Persia without a fight, which could indicate the rulers realized they were overpowered and outnumbered. However, ancient Greek historians like the legendary Herodotus, who, while prone to exaggeration is also a great source for ancient accounts of empires, indicates there was a siege. To further complicate matters, Abrahamic religious texts like the Torah and Bible state that Babylon fell after a single night's worth of battle, which resulted in the death of Prince Belshazzar.

Which is true?

When historians and archaeologists are faced with these many disparate accounts, especially when examining ancient history, the truth can often be found somewhere in the middle. Each of the three sources of information possess inherent flaws that need to be addressed, which is a common practice for historians no matter what era they study. Ancient tablets tend to be heavily skewed in favor of the king who ordered their creation, Greek historians liked to exaggerate and make fantastic stories, and religious texts cannot be considered historical canon without evidence for a combination of the last two reasons.

Keeping all of this in mind, what likely happened was a battle between the Persians and the Babylonians at a place called Opis where the Babylonians lost. Without the strength of the Babylonian army, many of the other major cities surrendered without fighting the invaders, and Nabonidus, who had been camped with his army in the south, most likely fled to Babylon or Borsippa. Belshazzar died in battle, and the governor of Assyria, a general named Gobryas, sided with the Persians, pursued Nabonidus, and killed him without the need to besiege any of the cities. As a reward, Cyrus named Gobryas the new governor of Babylon, which became a province in the Achaemenid Persian Empire.

Babylonia and Assyria in the Achaemenid Empire

The Assimilation of Babylonia

The Persians divided the Neo-Babylonian Empire into several separate provinces and colonies with the main two being Babylon and Assyria. Their gradual integration started around 539 BCE and would continue for centuries as Achaemenid Persia dominated the Mesopotamian landscape. Although the Babylonian elite grumbled at the thought of a new power, many commoners and disaffected ethnic or cultural groups within the territory rejoiced. One of Cyrus' first actions upon consolidating his rule was to allow foreign exiles to return to their homes. In particular, he allowed the thousands of Jews who had been abducted and forcibly sent from Judah to Babylon by Nebuchadnezzar II to return home. With them, they could bring their consecrated religious symbols, including images and vessels.

It's telling that Cyrus is referred to in Abrahamic religious texts as the liberator of the Jewish people and is one of the only non-believing individuals to be called a messiah. In biblical accounts, he is the man who releases the Jews from their Babylonian captivity. Although they would live under Persian rule for centuries, the Jews were able to return home and never officially rebelled or took up arms against their rulers.

Meanwhile, regular and native Babylonians still needed to be appeased. One of their greatest laws was that none could claim the right to rule over the territory until he had been consecrated into the office by the high priests. To appease this faction, Cyrus went through with the consecration, took the title of the King of Babylon, and justified his rule by claiming to be the successor of the original Babylonian kings and chosen by the patron deity Marduk to restore justice, order, and peace to southern Mesopotamia. Through this system, Cyrus managed to keep the peace and appease the priesthood of Marduk until his death.

Darius, Unrest, and Decline

Peace remained in Babylonia until roughly 521 BCE. By this time, Cyrus the Great and his son, Cambyses II, were both deceased and a new claimant to the throne emerged—Darius I. Darius I came to power in 522 BCE after defeating a usurper who had killed Cambyses and attempted to gain control of the empire. Darius I, also called Darius the Great, saw no reason to appease the Babylonians and abandoned the "chosen by Marduk" narrative in favor of pushing forward the Zoroastrian religion. Zoroastrianism is a monotheistic faith, meaning it has one god, and identifies the duality of good and evil. Good will eventually triumph over and destroy evil, and there was a single supreme being of wisdom whom the Persians worshipped. While this wasn't the sole reason for a Babylonian revolt, it did destroy Persian claims to legitimacy.[41]

---

[41] Aubrey Sélincourt, *The Histories*, (London: Penguin Classics, 2002).

A Frieze of Darius I's Palace in Susa

Once Darius I came into power, Babylonia tried to assert its independence under a new ruler called Nebuchadnezzar III—readers will note the originality here. Nebuchadnezzar III ruled for less than a year before the Persians appeared and put down the rebellion in spectacular, bloody fashion. At the same time, Darius I held off similar revolts throughout the empire and reconquered Assyria. Six years later in 514 BCE, the Babylonians once again declared independence, this time under the leadership of an Armenian man named Arakha, who renamed himself Nebuchadnezzar IV. Darius I reclaimed the territory once again and partly destroyed Babylon's walls during the siege. These would not be rebuilt.

Here, the story of Babylonia grows complacent. There were no more major revolts or revolutions for the next two centuries, and the city of Babylon slowly lost its importance and luster as peoples left and moved to the greater cultural capitals of the Persian Empire. Around 331 BCE, the Macedonians fought and kicked out the Persians, led by one of the grandest names in history—Alexander the Great. Alexander would die in Babylon in 323 BCE, most likely due to typhoid fever, although some believe he may have been poisoned. Once Alexander's former generals went to war, Babylonia and Assyria became a part of the Seleucid Empire, still controlled by the Macedonians.[42]

Babylonia lost its importance, although urban life continued much the same as it had for centuries well into the 1st century BCE. The region would be absorbed again and again into new empires, states, and countries, but never again would it claim independence.

The final fall of Babylon was complete.

---

[42] Ibid.

Chapter 10 – Religion, Mythology, and the Creation Myths

The religion of the Babylonians was that of Mesopotamia. The region possessed a cohesive cosmology, mythology, and structure of deities which were passed down over centuries. No matter what culture reigned supreme, whether it be the Sumerians, Akkadians, or the official Babylonians, the religion remained almost exactly the same. This religion was polytheistic, meaning there was more than one deity. Deities tended to have different domains, or areas of the earth and heavens over which they possessed control. There could be a god of the harvest, a god of storms, a goddess of fertility, or a goddess of love, among many others.

Since religion stayed similar over millennia, this chapter provides an overview of major developments that occurred within the Mesopotamian religion, including changes under the Neo-Babylonian Empire. A brief overview of what happened to the religion once the Hellenistic Period arrived is additionally included. Afterward, there is a description of several of the major deities.

The Mesopotamians

The Mesopotamian religion, as it relates to the Babylonians, started with the Sumerians. As mentioned many chapters ago, the Sumerians were the precursors to the official Babylonians which heavily influenced the culture, religion, politics, and economy of their successors. Many ethnic Sumerians would eventually become Babylonians as the people stayed within Mesopotamia. The

Sumerians possessed a theocratic society, or one ruled by religious tenets, beliefs, and usually a class of priests or other spiritual leaders. Sumerians were so dedicated to their religion and mythology that almost every aspect of life was seen to have been governed by one of the deities.

Before a kingship developed in Sumer, there were the theocratic city-states with ruling priests. The most significant cultural buildings were temples. Originally, these structures were constructed from simple stone and consisted of a single room for worship. As time went on, the buildings morphed into the legendary ziggurats. A ziggurat was a tall tower with a central sanctuary at the very top. It was not a triangle but instead consisted of multiple terraced levels with broad stairs which could be climbed to reach the sanctuary.

A Computer-Generated Model of a Ziggurat

These ziggurats were not public. Sumerians believed them to be the dwelling places of the gods, so access was forbidden for the majority of the population. Some professionals speculate that part of the design, with its numerous levels, was so guards could be posted around the stairwells to keep the common folk from spying on religious rites and ceremonies. Each Sumerian city possessed a patron deity whose rites and rituals would be performed more often than others. There exists one major, well-preserved ziggurat still in existence: the Chogha Zanbil in Iran.

Almost all Sumerian myths were passed down through an elaborate oral tradition. An oral tradition is one where members of a culture learn about their people's history, stories, and religion through storytelling, or one person relating the tales to another. Written accounts didn't appear until the end of the Early Dynastic Period around 2600 BCE. These writings, in addition to the oral tradition, helped preserve Sumerian religion when their power waned.

When the Akkadians started to displace the Sumerians, they adapted Sumerian religious beliefs into their own pantheon, where they were combined with preexisting rhetoric and ideas. Unfortunately for historians, archaeologists, and other individuals interested in culture, many of the original Akkadian beliefs have been lost to time. What is known is that many of the major Sumerian deities absorbed the spots held by their Akkadian counterparts and developed new names. For example, the Sumerian god An became the Akkadian god Anu with the same backstory, domain, and chief cities of worship.

Finally, the Babylonians emerged. The Amorite Babylonians actually kept many of the traditional Sumerian and Akkadian deities but made several major changes to the pantheon. In particular, they added the god Marduk and ordained him as the head of the pantheon. The original goddess Inanna's role was also transferred to a new deity called Ishtar. Otherwise, the world remained the same, and the Babylonians preserved the Sumerian and Akkadian languages for the purpose of worship.

The Mesopotamian Creation Myth

There are several Mesopotamian creation myths, or stories which focus on how the earth, heavens, and humans came to be. The main two are called "The Eridu Genesis" and "Enûma Eliš." The first is Sumerian and the second is Babylonian, but there are many more that describe smaller acts of creation. Some of these others are the "Debate Between Sheep and Grain," "Song of the Hoe," and "Debate Between Summer and Winter." It's a common theme throughout the myths where origin stories are told during conversations between personified objects, animals, seasons, and other inanimate creations.

The earliest Sumerian creation myth comes from a clay tablet discovered by archaeologists during an excavation in Nippur. The document appears to be from 1600 BCE, indicating that it was recorded late in the time of the Sumerians. Historian Thorkild Jacobsen named the tablet "The Eridu Genesis" myth and translated the cuneiform. Because of the advanced age of the relic, several pieces are missing or the inscription has been worn away by the literal sands of time. However, contemporary audiences can still piece together the rudimentary story. It goes as follows:

Nintur was paying attention:

Let me bethink myself of my humankind,

all forgotten as they are;

and mindful of mine,

Nintur's creatures let me bring them back

let me lead the people back from their trails.

May they come and build cities and cult places,

that I may cool myself in their shade;

may they lay the bricks for the cult cities in pure spots

and may they found places for divination in pure spots!

She gave directions for purification and cries for clemency,

the things that cool divine wrath,

perfected the divine service and the august offices,

said to the surrounding regions: "Let me institute peace there!"

When An, Enlil, Enki and Ninhursaga

fashioned the dark-headed people (a name the Sumerians gave themselves)

they had made the small animals that come up from out of the earth,

come from the earth in abundance

and had let there be, as it befits it, gazelles

wild donkeys, and four-footed beasts in the desert.

...and let me have him advise;
let me have him oversee their labor,
and let him teach the nation to follow along
unerringly like cattle!

When the royal scepter was coming down from heaven,
the august crown and the royal throne being already
down from heaven,
he (the king) regularly performed to perfection
the august divine services and offices,
laid the bricks of those cities in pure spots.
They were named by name and allotted half-bushel baskets.

The firstling of those cities, Eridu,
she gave to the leader Nudimmud,
the second, Bad-Tibira, she gave to the prince and the sacred one,
the third, Larak, she gave to Pabilsag,
the fourth, Sippar, she gave to the gallant Utu.
The fifth, Shuruppak, she gave to Ansud.

These cities, which had been named by names,
and had been allotted half-bushel baskets,
dredged the canals, which were blocked with purplish
wind-borne clay, and they carried water.
Their cleaning of the smaller canals

established abundant growth.[43]

A piece is missing here which describes how the noise created by the humans and their cities annoyed the chief god, Enlil, so greatly that he decided to eliminate the Sumerians entirely. He persuaded the divine assembly of the various deities to vote for human destruction through a massive storm that would flood the world. Savvy students of history, mythology, or religion will note the parallel of Sumerian legend with numerous others around the world.

The deluge myth, or the idea that the gods sent a great flood to wipe out humanity, appears in almost every major religion discovered across the globe, including Christianity, Hinduism, ancient Chinese mythology, ancient Norse mythology, ancient Greek mythology, Mayan mythology, the Lac Courte Oreilles Ojibwa tribe, the Aboriginals of Australia, and numerous other indigenous tribes throughout both American continents. The Mesopotamian flood myths, or those belonging to the Sumerians, future Babylonians, and others, are among the first.

Anthropologists suspect that these first renderings and writings of religion spread beyond Mesopotamia and influenced numerous other cultures across the combined landmass of Africa, Asia, and Europe, but it doesn't explain how it crossed the Atlantic, Pacific, and Indian Oceans unless the theory of gargantuan land bridges is true. Others, in particular the scholars of geology and the evolution of the planet, believe that something of climatological significance must have happened during humanity's earliest years, causing it to be recorded. No matter what the case may be, the Sumerian creation myth continues.

That day Nintur wept over her creatures

and holy Inanna was full of grief over their people;

but Enki took counsel with his own heart.

An, Enlil, Enki, and Ninhursaga

had the gods of heaven and earth swear

by the names of An and Enlil.

---

[43] Thorkild Jacobsen, "*The Harps That Once...: Sumerian Poetry in Translation*," (Yale University Press, Publishers, 1987).

At that time, Ziusudra was king

and lustration priest.

He fashioned, being a seer, the god of giddiness

and stood in awe beside it, wording his wishes humbly.

As he stood there regularly day after day

something that was not a dream was appearing:

conversation

a swearing of oaths by heaven and earth,

a touching of throats

and the gods bringing their thwarts up to Kiur.

And as Ziusudra stood there beside it, he went on hearing:

Step up to the wall to my left and listen!

Let me speak a word to you at the wall

and may you grasp what I say,

may you heed my advice!

By our hand a flood will sweep over

the cities of the half-bushel baskets, and the country;

the decision, that mankind is to be destroyed

has been made.

A verdict, a command of the assembly cannot be revoked,

an order of An and Enlil is not known

ever to have been countermanded,

their kingship, their term, has been uprooted

they must bethink themselves of that.

Now...

What I have to say to you...[44]

The part that is next missing appears to have been advice from the trickster deity, Enki, to build a boat and fill it with a male and female pair of each of the animals upon the earth. Readers will once again note the parallels between this deluge myth and others, including the biblical story of Noah and the Ark. Ziusudra, the king, obeys and manages to save humanity and the animals from the flood, but Enki's plan is discovered when Enlil finds the survivors. He is about to massacre them when Enki convinces the counsel of the divine to spare humanity. The story ends with two stanzas of verse which explain how Ziusudra ascended in the hierarchy of the heavens and the Sumerians were spared.

You here have sworn

by the life's breath of heaven

the life's breath of earth

that he verily is allied with yourself;

you there, An and Enlil,

have sworn by the life's breath of heaven,

the life's breath of earth.

That he is allied with all of you.

He will disembark the small animals

that come up from the earth!

Ziusudra, being king,

stepped up before An and Enlil

kissing the ground.

And An and Enlil after honoring him

were granting him life like a god's,

were making lasting breath of life, like a god's,

---

[44] Ibid.

descend into him.

That day they made Ziusudra,

preserver, as king, of the name of the small

animals and the seed of mankind,

live toward the east over the mountains

in mount Dilmun.[45]

Many of the significant Mesopotamian deities appear in this myth. Chief among the pantheon were An and Enlil, believed to have created the heavens and skies. The Mesopotamian gods were not human, and representations tended to make them anthropomorphic. Each one was a being of tremendous size, similar to a giant, with unfathomable power. Stone carvings and depictions showed the deities wearing horned caps at all times and special *melam* capable of inspiring terror and awe in any mortal who saw it.

The Babylonian Creation Myth

Historians place the development of the Babylonian creation myth, the "Enûma Eliš," to the time of Hammurabi, or around the 1700s BCE. There are several versions of the story, but the most well-preserved dates around the 7th century BCE and comes from the Library of Ashurbanipal. It's inscribed in seven tablets and varies significantly from the original Sumerian creation myth, but presents similar themes and ideas. An excerpt from the translated first tablet is shown below:

Tablet I

When the heavens above did not exist,

And earth beneath had not come into being —

There was Apsû, the first in order, their begetter,

And demiurge Tia-mat, who gave birth to them all;

They had mingled their waters together

Before meadow-land had coalesced and reed-bed was to be found —

When not one of the gods had been formed

---

45 Ibid.

Or had come into being, when no destinies had been decreed,

The gods were created within them:

Lah-mu and Lah-amu were formed and came into being.

While they grew and increased in stature

Anšar and Kišar, who excelled them, were created.

They prolonged their days, they multiplied their years.

Anu, their son, could rival his fathers.

Anu, the son, plendo Anšar,

And Anu begat Nudimmud, his own equal.

Nudimmud was the champion among his fathers:

Profoundly discerning, wise, of robust strength;

Very much stronger than his father's begetter, Anšar

He had no rival among the gods, his brothers.

The divine brothers came together,

Their clamour got loud, throwing Tia-mat into a turmoil.

They jarred the nerves of Tia-mat,

And by their dancing they spread alarm in Anduruna.

Apsû did not diminish their clamour,

And Tia-mat was silent when confronted with them.

Their conduct was displeasing to her,

Yet though their plendor was not good, she wished to spare them.[46]

The first tablet covers the creation of literally everything, for before Apsû and Tiamat there was nothing. From these two original deities came others, who disturbed Tiamat. To fight against them, Tiamat proposed the creation of monsters that would stop the direction in which the universe was moving. The following five tablets detail how her plan would not come to fruition as several of the younger

---

[46] W.G. Lambert, *Mesopotamian Creation Stories*, (European History and Culture E-Books Online, 2007).

gods plot against her. Marduk is made the new overlord of all of the deities, slays Tiamat by bashing her skull in with a mace, and uses her body to create the heavens and earth as humans know it. Marduk then goes about creating humans by sacrificing one of the other gods and using their blood to form the first Babylonians. At this point, the creation story ends with an entire tablet dedicated to praising Marduk and reading fifty of his numerous names, which indicates just how central to Babylonian religion this god was. Part of the translated text of Tablet VII is included here so readers get an idea of all of the things that were attributed to this single deity.

Tablet VII

Asarre, the giver of arable land who established plough-land,

The creator of barley and flax, who made plant life grow.

Asaralim, who is revered in the counsel chamber, whose counsel excels,

The gods heed it and grasp fear of him.

Asaralimnunna, the noble, the light of the father, his begetter,

Who directs the decrees of Anu, Enlil, and Ea, that is Ninšiku.

He is their provisioner, who assigns their incomes,

Whose turban multiplies abundance for the land.

Tutu is he, who accomplishes their renovation,

Let him purify their sanctuaries that they may repose.

Let him fashion an incantation that the gods may rest,

Though they rise up in fury, let them withdraw.

He is indeed exalted in the assembly of the gods, his [fathers],

No one among the gods can [equal] him.

Tutu-Ziukkinna, the life of [his] host,

Who established, the pure heavens for the gods,

Who took charge of their courses, who appointed [their stations],

May he not be forgotten among mortals, but [let them remember] his deeds.

Tutu-Ziku they called him thirdly, the establisher of purification,

The god of the pleasant breeze, lord of success and obedience,

Who produces bounty and wealth, who establishes abundance,

Who turns everything scant that we have into profusion,

Whose pleasant breeze we sniffed in time of terrible trouble,

Let men command that his praises be constantly uttered, let them offer worship to

him.

Marduk thus took his place at the head of the Babylonian pantheon, rising above many of the other deities. Other gods of note were individuals like Ishtar and Nergal, who controlled love, war, sexuality, and the underworld. In particular, Ishtar possessed one of the largest cults in Babylonia and was considered the principal goddess for women, marriage, and childbirth in addition to being a fierce, warlike deity. Nergal, meanwhile, represented fire and the desert in addition to the underworld, and frequently appeared as a lion in his depictions. In contrast to the popular Greek myth of Hades and Persephone, Nergal was not the original god of the underworld but actually married Ereshkigal, who shared her power with him. Nergal could not stay the entire year and would leave for six months at a time, demonstrating the changing of the seasons.[47]

---

[47] "Nergal" *The Ancient History Encyclopedia,* https://www.ancient.eu/Nergal/.

Chapter 11 – The Short Version of the Biblical Babylonians

Babylon frequently appears in the Abrahamic religions as a symbol of decadence and sin. When referenced in documents like the Bible, it's important to realize that different passages are referring to the Babylonian Empire and to the city of Babylon itself, although both possessed the same connotations. The primary reason for the presence of Babylonia in these documents is the perpetual struggle that existed between the Babylonians and the Jewish people, who lived to the west in a region known as the Levant. During the second and first millennia BCE, the Jewish people attempted to form their own kingdoms but were frequently overrun, conquered, and turned into vassals by their more powerful neighbors. At one point, these conquerors were the kings of the Neo-Babylonian Empire, who uprooted thousands of the Jewish people from their homes following a rebellion and forced them to live in Babylonia as captives.

This action became known in religious texts as the Babylonian captivity. Once the Neo-Babylonian Empire fell to the Persians and Cyrus the Great, the Jewish people were able to return home and wrote about their experiences in Babylonia in their religious documents. Now, it's important to realize once more that historians and archaeologists cannot accept documents like the Torah or Bible as fact simply because the physical historical evidence does not exist. This does not mean that Judaism or Christianity is not true, but it does color the perception of events. For the purposes of this chapter, what was written in the documents of Abrahamic religions needs to be taken with a grain of salt as the religious texts were repeatedly edited by the kings, high priests, and nobility to reiterate the Israelite belief that they were God's chosen people, that the nobles and kings possessed a divine right to rule, and that the Babylonians were clearly a sinful people being punished for daring to act against the Jewish people.

The Fall of Babylon, 1453 Woodcut

The Babylonian Captivity

Keeping all of this in mind, Abrahamic religious documents tell a different story of the Babylonian captivity than that explained by historic sources as seen in previous chapters. According to the Bible, the situation went something like this:

> The word that came to Jeremiah concerning all the people of Judah, in the fourth year of King Jehoiakim son of Josiah of Judah (that was the first year of King Nebuchadnezzar of Babylon), which the prophet Jeremiah spoke to all the people of Judah and all the inhabitants of Jerusalem:

> For twenty-three years, from the thirteenth year of King Josiah son of Amon of Judah, to this day, the word of the Lord has come to me, and I have spoken persistently to you, but you have not listened.

> And though the Lord persistently sent you all his servants the prophets, you have neither listened nor inclined your ears to

hear when they said, "Turn now, every one of you, from your evil way and wicked doings, and you will remain upon the land that the Lord has given to you and your ancestors from of old and forever; do not go after other gods to serve and worship them, and do not provoke me to anger with the work of your hands. Then I will do you no harm."

Yet you did not listen to me, says the Lord, and so you have provoked me to anger with the work of your hands to your own harm.

Therefore thus says the Lord of hosts: Because you have not obeyed my words, I am going to send for all the tribes of the north, says the Lord, even for King Nebuchadrezzar of Babylon, my servant, and I will bring them against this land and its inhabitants, and against all these nations around; I will utterly destroy them, and make them an object of horror and of hissing, and an everlasting disgrace.

And I will banish from them the sound of mirth and the sound of gladness, the voice of the bridegroom and the voice of the bride, the sound of the millstones and the light of the lamp.

This whole land shall become a ruin and a waste, and these nations shall serve the king of Babylon seventy years.

Then after seventy years are completed, I will punish the king of Babylon and that   nation, the land of the Chaldeans, for their iniquity, says the Lord, making the land an everlasting waste.

I will bring upon that land all the words that I have uttered against it, everything written in this book, which Jeremiah prophesied against all the nations.

For many nations and great kings shall make slaves of them also; and I will repay them according to their deeds and the work of their hands.[48]

In this version of events, the Israelite god is punishing the people for their sins and failure to uphold the tenets of worship properly. The

---

[48] Bible, Jeremiah 25

Neo-Babylonian Empire is sent to remove the Jewish people from their homeland where they can suffer until a time comes when they may return to their territory once more as God's chosen people. This text then places the Persians in the role of liberators, once more sent by God specifically to aid the Jewish people while ignoring the geopolitical intricacies unfolding in the region. Babylon, meanwhile, is destroyed for being sinful and failing to worship the proper deity.

James Tissot, The Flight of the Prisoners

The Whore of Babylon

The other major instance of Babylon appearing in Abrahamic religious texts is the strange tale of the Whore of Babylon, who remains an iconic figure in Western civilization. She was a symbolic figure meant to represent evil and the temptations experienced by humans while on earth. She appears in the Book of Revelations in the following passage:

Then one of the seven angels who had the seven bowls came and said to me, "Come, I will show you the judgment of the great prostitute who is seated on many waters,

with whom the kings of the earth have committed sexual immorality, and with the wine of whose sexual immorality the dwellers on earth have become drunk."

And he carried me away in the Spirit into a wilderness, and I saw a woman sitting on a scarlet beast that was full of blasphemous names, and it had seven heads and ten horns.

The woman was arrayed in purple and scarlet, and adorned with gold and jewels and pearls, holding in her hand a golden cup full of abominations and the impurities of her sexual immorality.

And on her forehead was written a name of mystery: "Babylon the great, mother of prostitutes and of earth's abominations.[49]

The Whore of Babylon is frequently associated with the Antichrist as well as the Beast of Revelation. She is not a real person so much as a representation of idolatry and other major sins which would keep practitioners of Judaism and Christianity out of Heaven. Historians and theologians alike speculate that she is associated with Babylon because of the aforementioned Babylonian captivity and previous comparisons that indicate Babylon equals sin and excess.

---

[49] Bible, Revelations 1-5

The Whore of Babylon Atop the Seven-Headed Beast

Conclusion – The Legacy of the Babylonians

So, why should a contemporary audience care about the Babylonians?

It can be difficult for modern individuals to realize how much the actions of civilizations from thousands of years ago impact their lives in the present day. The Babylonians were responsible for several major scientific breakthroughs, including new mathematical methods for understanding the cosmos and creating calendars. They charted the stars, discovered new building materials, and laid the foundations for other civilizations like the Greeks and Romans, who continue to be upheld by Western civilizations as the great forebearers of contemporary political and social intellectualism.

Like many of the other Mesopotamian civilizations, the Babylonians advanced agriculture, metallurgy, warfare, and other essential practices so humans didn't have to start over again every time a new people tried to develop their own culture. Frequent warfare and trade with other civilizations throughout the Near East, Asia Minor, and northern Africa also meant culture, religion, and techniques could travel great distances.

Babylon or Babylonia even had a great effect on the development of the Abrahamic religions, as there would be no captivity narrative without them!

Even if someone doesn't care too much about these vital essentials, they can still appreciate the complexity of a culture that survived for multiple millennia and spawned beautiful artwork, intricate religion and worship, and unique laws and the basis for future legal systems around the world. After all, it was Hammurabi who came up with the infamous "an eye for an eye" viewpoint for examining the world and justice.

Keeping all of this in mind, it would be difficult to imagine a world without the Babylonians. History is very much a tapestry: If someone pulls out one thread, the entire thing starts to unravel. This is the position of the Babylonians: A crucial thread that can't be removed without dismantling the course of human civilization as the contemporary world knows it.

Here are some other books by Captivating History that we think you would find interesting

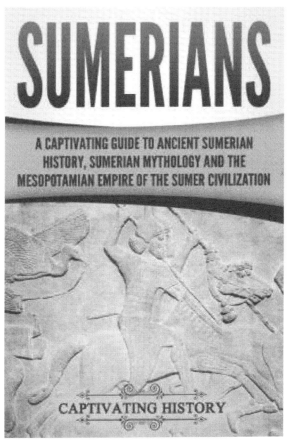

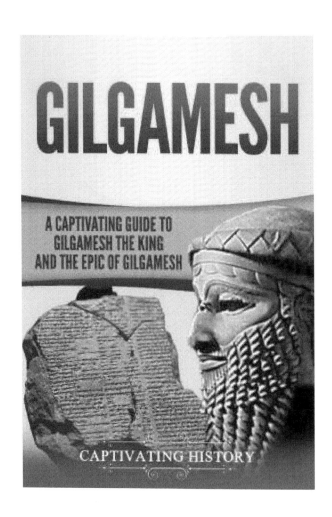

Free Bonus from Captivating History (Available for a Limited time)

Hi History Lovers!

Now you have a chance to join our exclusive history list so you can get your first history ebook for free as well as discounts and a potential to get more history books for free! Simply visit the link below to join.

Captivatinghistory.com/ebook

Also, make sure to follow us on Facebook, Twitter and Youtube by searching for Captivating History.

References and Further Reading

Arnold, Bill T. *Who Were the Babylonians?* Atlanta: The Society of Biblical Literature, 2004.

Bottéro, Jean. *Mesopotamia: Writing, Reasoning and the Gods.* New York: St. Martin's Press, 2012.

Bryce, Trevor. *Babylonia: A Very Short Introduction.* Oxford: Oxford University Press, 2016.

Crawford, Harriett. *Sumer and the Sumerians.* New York: Cambridge University Press, 2004.

Elayi, Josette. *The History of Phoenicia.* Lockwood Press, 2018.

Foster, Benjamin R. *The Age of Agade: Inventing Empire in Ancient Mesopotamia.* New York: Routledge Publishing, 2016.

Grayson, A. Kirk. *Assyrian Rulers of the Early First Millennium BCE (1114-859 BC).* Toronto: University of Toronto Press, 1991.

Houston, Mary G. *Ancient Egyptian, Mesopotamian & Persian Costume.* London: A. & C. Black, 1954.

Jacobsen, Thorkild. *"The Harps That Once...: Sumerian Poetry in Translation."* Yale University Press, 1987.

King, L. W. *Chronicles concerning early Babylonian kings: including records of the early history of the Kassites and the country of the sea.* London: Luzac and co., 2014.

Kriwaczek, Paul. *Babylon: Mesopotamia and the Birth of Civilization.* New York: St. Martin's Press, 2012.

Lambert, W. G. *Mesopotamian Creation Stories.* European History and Culture E-Books Online, 2007.

Mitchell, Stephen. *Gilgamesh: A New English Version.* New York: Free Press, 2004.

Sayce, Rev. A. H., Professor of Assyriology, Oxford, "The Archaeology of the Cuneiform Inscriptions." *Society for Promoting Christian Knowledge.* New York: 1908.

Schneider, Adam W. and Adali, Selim F. ""No harvest was reaped:" demographic and climate factors in the decline of the Neo-Assyrian Empire." *Climate Change* 127, no. 3, 2014: 435-446.

Stol, Marten. *Women in the Ancient Near East.* Boston: De Gruyter, 2016.

Sélincourt, Aubrey. *The Histories.* London: Penguin Classics, 2002.

Shamsabad, Cameron. *History's Forgotten Father: Cyrus the Great.* Shamsabad Publishing, 2014.

Van De Mieroop, Marc. *King Hammurabi of Babylon: A Biography.* Malden: Blackwell Publishing, 2005.

Yirdirim, Kemal. *The Ancient Amorites (Amurru) of Mesopotamia.* LAP Lambert Academic Publishing, 2017.

Made in the USA
Middletown, DE
03 November 2020

23278498R00064